"Reading *In Touch* is a remarkable journey through the body into a wholeness of Being. A gifted clinician and dedicated spiritual practitioner, John Prendergast guides us in a powerful process of inner attunement, one that unfolds into deep realization and full, embodied aliveness."

TARA BRACH, PHD, author of *Radical Acceptance* and *True Refuge*

"*In Touch* offers a powerful and practical exploration of the often confusing and seemingly conflicting reality of the vital importance of being 'in touch' with both an internal bodily sense of ourselves and the equally crucial interconnected self that is a part of a much larger whole beyond the boundaries of the skin. John Prendergast's decades of clinical work as well as his personal experiences provide an intriguing set of observations that will stimulate reflections on who you really are and how to best wed these dual realities of identity. Soak in these words of wisdom and you may just find your 'self' opening to the exciting liberation that emerges when inner and interconnected self are integrated into a coherent, flourishing whole."

DANIEL J. SIEGEL, MD, director of the Mindsight Institute, clinical professor at UCLA School of Medicine, and author of *Mindsight, Brainstorm, The Mindful Brain, The Mindful Therapist, Pocket Guide to Interpersonal Neurobiology,* and *The Developing Mind*

"Whether making important decisions or sensing what will best serve us, we have all the love and wisdom we need right inside of us. *In Touch* is the perfect guidebook to access this 'inner knowing,' which will connect you to your deepest truth. John Prendergast's beautiful book is insightful, practical, and full of heart. I highly recommend it."

JAMES BARAZ, coauthor of *Awakening Joy* and cofounding teacher of Spirit Rock Meditation Center

"Psychotherapist and spiritual mentor John Prendergast has written a beautiful, inspiring book that helps us tune in to our deepest nature so that we can sense and decode subtle body-sensed information that enables us to 'more gracefully navigate life and to awaken.' Drawing from his extensive experience as spiritual practitioner, psychotherapist, and teacher, John Prendergast integrates strands of contemporary psychological theory and esoteric spiritual teaching brilliantly, bringing depth and maturity to this work, yet making it accessible and easy to understand. Interwoven throughout are 'experiments' that invite us to explore for ourselves the concepts so clearly described. I will recommend *In Touch* to my friends, colleagues, and my EMDR students as a helpful guide for how to connect with their inner knowing and unfolding of True Self."

LAUREL PARNELL, PHD, author of *Attachment-Focused EMDR, Tapping In, A Therapist's Guide to EMDR, EMDR in the Treatment of Adults Abused as Children*, and *Transforming Trauma: EMDR*

"In this remarkable book, Dr. Prendergast opens up the enormous potential of subtle body awareness as a vital instrument in allowing us to feel into the innermost spiritual and psychological realities of our own and others' existence. This book is essential reading for everyone who aspires to meet others in a spirit of loving care and boundless intimacy. It is stunning in the territory it covers in detailing a new cartography of embodied awareness. Dr. Prendergast shows how deep somatic sensitivity and empathic resonance ultimately rely on the clean-clear presencing of nondual awareness. This book is a must-read."

PETER FENNER, PHD, author of *Radiant Mind* and *Natural Awakening*

"In this lucid, comprehensive, groundbreaking book, master psychotherapist and spiritual teacher John Prendergast shows us how to listen to our elusive inner wisdom as a path not only to psychological healing but also to the realization of our nondual spiritual nature. Informed by the author's 30 years of experience as a guide on the journey of greater authenticity and inner alignment, and illuminated by the teachings of Advaita Vedanta and by the latest neuroscience, *In Touch* is a must-read for everyone who aspires to realize and live from the truth of their being, beyond the mind."

STEPHAN BODIAN, author of *Meditation for Dummies* and *Beyond Mindfulness*

"This guide to the process of listening within is clear and practical, while also helping the reader plumb the multidimensional depths and nuances of the inner journey. Highly recommended."

JOHN WELWOOD, PHD, author of *Toward a Psychology of Awakening*

"John Prendergast is a master psychotherapist, teacher, spiritual guide, and author whose groundbreaking new work, *In Touch,* reveals the critical role our bodies play as a vital source of inner knowing and self-trust. Drawing from decades of intimate work with clients and students, Dr. Prendergast clearly and at times poetically describes the art of tuning in to the body's wisdom as a guide to navigate daily life as well as to discover our deepest nature. Filled with keen insight, inspiring stories, and potent exercises, *In Touch* is a treasure and pleasure to read—a seminal work."

RICHARD MILLER, PHD, clinical psychologist, researcher, yogic scholar, spiritual teacher, and author of *The iRest Program for Healing PTSD* and *Yoga Nidra*

"While there are a number of books about tapping into our inner wisdom, *In Touch* offers a depth of exploration and clear practical guidance which makes it stand out. In particular, it helps us sort out the bodily promptings of the True-Self from the 'noise' of our habitual emotions, our expectations, and our fixed beliefs. It is a useful and powerful guide, both for beginners and those already committed to a path of inner exploration."

PETER A. LEVINE, PHD, bestselling author of *Waking the Tiger, Healing Trauma,* and the video course *Healing Trauma*

"*In Touch* synthesizes essential insights in the fields of spirituality, psychology, and embodiment that could only be written by someone who walks their talk. John Prendergast's lifetime of dedication to the spiritual path and decades of dedicated work as a psychotherapist shine through these pages and offer a rare degree of both subtlety and accessibility. We are fortunate to have this book available to us!"

MARIANA CAPLAN, PHD, psychotherapist and author of six books in the field of psychology and spirituality, including *Eyes Wide Open* and *Halfway Up the Mountain*

"Although it may seem a rare and elusive task at first, it is entirely possible to learn to relax the subtle contractions that disconnect us from our embodied awareness. John Prendergast has long studied the epic journey from abstracted head to wise, embodied heart. In this book, he is a compassionate friend to the reader, showing step by step what is possible and real. Each word is spoken authentically and with care. This book will teach you how to drop in and to get 'in actual touch' with your always already sanity and joy. What a gift!"

TERRY PATTEN, coauthor of *Integral Life Practice* and creator and host of *Beyond Awakening*

"John Prendergast is a leading voice on the emerging interface between therapy and nonduality. His approach to therapy in general and the body in particular is deeply informed by his experiential understanding of nonduality, and his approach to nonduality is grounded in the felt and lived experience of the body and world. As such, *In Touch* is an insightful and heartfelt meditation for anyone who seeks not only to realize the essential, unconditioned nature of themselves but to live its implications fully in all realms of experience."

RUPERT SPIRA, teacher of nonduality and author of *The Transparency of Things*, *Presence*, *The Ashes of Love*, and *The Light of Pure Knowing*

"*In Touch* is a beautifully written book that navigates the reader through the inner multisensory world of all knowing. With grace and love, John Prendergast has created a masterpiece."

MARIE MANUCHEHRI, RN, author of *Intuitive Self-Healing*

"A beautiful and undogmatic guide, rich and practical, to the ins and outs of waking up and waking down in the modern world. In a style that is scholarly yet deeply human and accessible, drawing from his many years of experience as a therapist and spiritual teacher, John Prendergast speaks of the deepest kind of healing: how a curious, self-shining awareness at the core of our experience is remembered and uncovered, then permeates through every layer of our body-minds, saturating every feeling and sensation, every crevice of our known world with light and understanding. This is an embodied awakening that leaves us not more detached from the world, but more intimate with the world than ever, more awake to the sacredness of every moment, to the gifts of being alive, to the preciousness of connection in all its forms. We wake up to unchanging awareness, and we wake down to the beauty and intelligence of our ever-changing bodies, and we finally discover how transparent we always were—how limitless, how vast, how free. This is an important book that will illuminate the way ahead for countless seekers of truth all over the world, and clear up many misunderstandings about the pathless path of awakening. With John, you are in safe hands. Highly recommended."

JEFF FOSTER, author of *The Deepest Acceptance* and
Falling in Love with Where You Are

"This is a beautifully written, accessible guide to deeper dimensions of self-knowledge and connection with other people. Supported by scientific research and decades of experience as a psychotherapist and spiritual teacher, John Prendergast shows us how listening to our body can increase our capacity for spaciousness, subtle attunement, love, and clarity. This is an intelligent, compassionate contribution to the new frontier of embodied psychological healing and spiritual awakening."

JUDITH BLACKSTONE, PHD, author of *Belonging Here,*
The Intimate Life, and *The Enlightenment Process*

"A remarkable book. John Prendergast's lifetime experience both as a psychotherapist and a spiritual practitioner gives us a much-needed map to explore our inner experience through listening to the signals of the physical body—a map that can guide us to a profound intimacy with ourselves and our own deep knowing."

ROGER HOUSDEN, author of *Keeping the Faith Without a Religion*

"This book is a wonderful tool to navigate your way to your inner self. Full of research, stories, guidance, and techniques, it is a vital and important contribution to the journey of self-knowledge and self-discovery. What a treasure!"

ED AND DEB SHAPIRO, authors of *Be the Change* and *The Bodymind Workbook*

"Dr. Prendergast walks us compassionately through the tricky terrain of the awakening process in this clear-eyed exploration of four somatic markers of an evolving consciousness. *In Touch* is an invaluable practical guide for those probing the depths and heights of what it means to be both truly divine and truly human."

MEG LUNDSTROM, author of *What To Do When You Can't Decide* and coauthor of *The Power of Flow*

in touch

in touch

How to Tune In to the
Inner Guidance of Your Body
and Trust Yourself

John J. Prendergast, PhD

Foreword by Rick Hanson, PhD
New York Times bestselling author of *Buddha's Brain* and *Hardwiring Happiness*

SOUNDS TRUE
BOULDER, COLORADO

Sounds True, Inc.
Boulder, CO 80306

This work is solely for personal growth and education. It should not be treated as a
substitute for professional assistance, therapeutic activities such as psychotherapy
or counseling, or medical advice. In the event of physical or mental distress,
please consult with appropriate health professionals. The application of protocols
and information in this book is the choice of each reader, who assumes full
responsibility for his or her understandings, interpretations, and results. The author
and publisher assume no responsibility for the actions or choices of any reader.

Cover design by Rachael Murray
Book design by Beth Skelley

Printed in the United States of America

Adapted Attachment Interview questions on pages 8–9 from *The Mindful Therapist:
A Clinician's Guide to Mindsight and Neural Integration* by Daniel J. Siegel.
Copyright © 2010 by Mind Your Brain, Inc. Used by permission of W. W. Norton
& Company, Inc.

"The Avowal" by Denise Levertov, from *Oblique Prayers,* copyright © 1984 by
Denise Levertov. Reprinted by permission of New Directions Publishing Corp.

"Last Night as I Was Sleeping" by Antonio Machado, from *Times Alone: Selected
Poems of Antonio Machado,* translated by Robert Bly (Middletown, Conn.:
Wesleyan University Press, 1983). Reprinted by permission of Robert Bly.

Rumi quote on page 150 from *Rumi: Gazing at the Beloved—The Radical Practice
of Beholding the Divine* by Will Johnson (Inner Traditions, 2003). Reprinted by
permission of Will Johnson.

Library of Congress Cataloging-in-Publication Data
Prendergast, John J., 1950–
    In touch : how to tune in to the inner guidance of your body and trust yourself /
John J. Prendergast, PhD ; foreword by Rick Hanson, PhD.
        pages cm
    Includes bibliographical references.
    ISBN 978-1-62203-207-5
    1. Self. 2. Self-acceptance. I. Title.
    BF697.P69487 2015
    158.1—dc23
                                    2014032736

Ebook ISBN 978-1-62203-449-9

10 9 8 7 6 5 4

To my special beloveds, Christiane and James
and
my teachers who illumined the way, Jean Klein and Adyashanti

contents

FOREWORD

by rick hanson, phd

Somewhere between conception and birth, inside the womb of your mother, you began to have an embodied sense of living: the feeling of your heart beating, of pressure against your skin, of discomfort and its relief. It has been said that ontogeny recapitulates phylogeny: the development of a human embryo contains within it the evolution of the human species. First and foremost, every animal—even the simplest worm—needs to know what's going on inside its body. Are the internal organs working? Is there hunger or thirst? Does anything hurt?

The internal sensing of the body—continually tracking what's happening "in here"—evolved long before the hearing and seeing that tell us about the world "out there." The neural architecture of this sensing is ancient and fundamental, and during your own development in utero, it was the basis for your very first experiences—and the first glimmerings of consciousness.

Because the state of the body is so fundamental to raw survival, most of the information entering your brain comes from the skin inward. This flow of information and related experiences brings a primal, *embodied* "feeling of being," as Antonio Damasio puts it. Meanwhile—both when you were still in the womb and then after your birth—there was a dawning awareness of an environment out there that moved and changed in ways distinct from the feeling of being in here. Repeated experiences of this difference between out there and in here gradually built up a core sense—initially entirely nonverbal—of "this-here-ness," "me-ness," identity.

In sum, your embodied experience of living—being in touch with yourself, as John Prendergast explores in this important book—is the fundamental basis for both consciousness and the sense of self.

Of course, this word *self* is a tricky one, and I mean it here as a particular body-mind process—as a *person*—without presuming that there exists a stable, unified entity somewhere inside looking out through the eyes. The common assumption in Western philosophy, psychology, and culture that there is such an "I" inside everyone is the source of much needless suffering and harm as we try to hold on, as this "I," to inherently impermanent experiences, glamorize and glorify it (look at me!), try to shield it from life's ups and downs, and take life personally. To be sure, resilience and well-being as a person support insight into the transient, compounded, insubstantial, "empty" nature of the apparent me-myself-and-I. One of the great strengths of Dr. Prendergast's approach is his balanced emphasis on both an opening *in* to an intimacy with this body's streaming of consciousness and an opening *out* to the sense of this streaming as no more than a momentary and local expression of the vast web of human culture, nature, and material reality—and of mysteries that transcend all of these.

Like other great teachers, the Buddha was interested in what was true, but he was more interested in what *helped*. In the same way, this book draws us into an intimacy with what is true about our experiencing; this felt clarity is interesting and illuminating in its own right, but more importantly, it is useful. It is useful for anyone, but especially for those who teach, raise, coach, or counsel others. We learn how to attune to four major ways to recognize when we are in touch with ourselves: relaxed groundedness, inner alignment, openheartedness, and spaciousness. With many experiential practices, specific methods, and tools for working with others, *In Touch* is that rare book combining both profound understanding and practical, down-to-earth benefits.

I've known John Prendergast for many years as his colleague, friend, and student. He is truly a master of his craft. Drawing upon neuroscience, clinical tools, nondual wisdom teachings, and his own genuine realization, he has pulled together the lessons of a lifetime in this extraordinary book. I commend it to your hands and to your heart.

INTRODUCTION

in touch with your inner knowing

Kelly and I had met for a number of sessions before. Today, after checking in briefly, we settled into a soft, noneffortful, meditative gazing and deep silence together. We both trusted that whatever needed attention would naturally arise.

Kelly had recently been rear-ended by a speeding van as she slowed for a pedestrian on a crosswalk. As a result of this serious accident, she had a number of physical symptoms, including neck pain and periodic migraine headaches. After a few minutes of sitting with me, she felt a knot of tension in her solar plexus. As she sensed into it, she wondered if there was some unconscious psychological reason she had had two fairly serious car accidents in the past year.

"Several of my friends have suggested this," she said. "But maybe it's just that shit happens?"

"Ah, self-doubt," I responded. "It is true that things happen for unknown reasons. Yet what is important is how we are with them, whether we create stories around them or not."

"I didn't realize that this was self-doubt, but I can see that this is what it is. Yes, I can see that this belief that I'm somehow creating these accidents is related to my early Christian upbringing that I'm being punished for doing something wrong. I can sense that this isn't true."

As this understanding came to Kelly, the knot of tension quickly dissolved and was replaced by a feeling of deep relaxation and openness. We then shared a palpable sense of being together in presence—individual, distinct, yet not essentially separate.

Internal body tension is often directly related to a conscious or subconscious limiting belief that we hold. A willingness to sense and feel a contraction, as well as to investigate the truth of an associated belief, allows the tension to transform and dissolve over time. Something in Kelly could sense the falsehood of her belief and could feel what was true for her, allowing her to return to her original openness. Kelly sensed her sensations, felt her feelings, questioned her beliefs, and eventually rested in and as her natural awareness.

What is this sense of inner knowing that Kelly experienced? We have all probably experienced it at some time or another—something just feels on or off the mark inside of us. It has been called many things: the small, still voice; a felt sense; intuition; heart or whole-body wisdom; somatic intelligence; a hunch; or a gut feeling. In Eastern contemplative traditions, it is called *prajna.*

Our inner knowing may be fleeting or quietly persistent, and it is more sensation than thought. We feel it somewhere deep inside of ourselves—often in the heart area or the belly. It doesn't explain or justify itself. It is frequently unbidden and unexpected. It can be deeply reassuring and soothing, or on occasion, it can be very unwelcome, rocking the boat, making waves, and turning our life upside down. Sometimes we may not want to know what we know—the truth can be very inconvenient. It can end marriages, friendships, and careers and disrupt families, spiritual communities, and governments. It is also very liberating to live in accord with this truth. It is a two-edged knife that cuts us out of our comfort zone and opens us to life as it is.

This book will help you recognize your own natural sense of inner knowing by showing you how to listen to your body for guidance and then follow it. Getting in touch with your inner knowing is a process of unlearning, letting go, and deeply attuning with yourself in a new way. It can help you navigate life's challenges more gracefully, authentically, and intimately. It can also help you discover who you really are.

Getting in touch with your inner knowing will ultimately lead you to experience your natural openness, as Kelly did at the end of her session. In this openness, the ordinary boundary of self and other softens and dissolves. This brings a sense of great inner freedom and deep intimacy. We are *free from* the story of who we think we are—especially from the core belief that we are a separate, isolated, and deficient self. We are also *free to* intimately experience our connection with the whole of life. Our deepest suffering comes from imagining and feeling that we are a separate self. Our inner knowing will eventually release us from this illusion.

My Own Journey

My passion for this subject—the sense of inner knowing—began during my boyhood. Between the ages of ten and thirteen, when I went to bed, I would sometimes drift into an altered and expansive state of consciousness where my body would alternately feel infinitely large or small. I never talked about these experiences with anyone and, in fact, forgot about them until I began a daily meditation practice in 1970, when I was in college. During my second meditation, I was quite surprised to briefly reconnect with this sense of the infinite.

After graduating from college and serving in the army in Germany as a Vietnam-era draftee, I became a Transcendental Meditation (TM) teacher and attended a series of long retreats in the Alps. During one of these retreats, I had a compelling inner vision of a powerful and controversial Indian teacher named Sai Baba. This vision, along with other factors, led me to leave the TM organization and head off to India two years later in search of a teacher. On my second visit to India in 1980, I had an unusually powerful dream during which I experienced an initial awakening of what I call the energy body—the body of subtle sensation.

I returned to the United States and started my doctoral studies in clinical psychology. As an intern sitting with clients, I began to directly feel, both emotionally and energetically, what my clients were describing, sometimes before they were aware of it themselves. I now understand this phenomenon as being part of empathic resonance. I kept my experiences to myself for several years, disclosing them to neither my clients nor my clinical supervisors. Nothing in my classes or readings had prepared me for this kind of direct, interpersonal experiencing. It took time for me to trust that I was accurately resonating with my clients. At the time, I was a bit astonished to experience this kind of interconnectedness. Now, over thirty years later, it seems normal and matter-of-fact.

Around this time I had a deeply touching dream with Nisarga-datta Maharaj, the feisty sage from Mumbai (formerly Bombay). In the dream Maharaj looked deeply in my eyes with great lucidity and then took my arm and told me that I could spend some time with him. Following that dream, I immediately read Maharaj's famous dialogues, mostly with young Westerners, entitled *I Am That*. His book made a very deep impression on me and reoriented my spiritual search towards self-inquiry.

In 1983, I met the European Advaita master Jean Klein while he was teaching in the Bay Area, and I *knew* that he was my teacher. I studied closely with him until his death fifteen years later. In addition to offering dialogues that encouraged a deep listening and self-investigation, Jean taught a very subtle form of yoga that was influenced by Kashmiri Shaivism. It involved a slow and careful body sensing that further catalyzed my native sensitivity. During those years with Jean, I would occasionally be awakened after two hours of deep sleep by various knots in the energy body working themselves out. These workouts left me exhausted and drained in the morning.

When Jean died in 1998, I thought I was done with teachers and just needed to cook on my own. However, a year later I met a relatively young Californian named Adyashanti. Much to my surprise, I sensed the same radiant presence and beautiful clarity in Adya, as he is called, as I did in Jean, despite marked differences in their ages, personalities, backgrounds, and teaching styles. However, a certain loyalty to Jean made me keep my distance from Adya until I was invited by a friend to attend a small private retreat at the base of Mount Whitney, in the eastern Sierras, in 2001.

During an exchange with Adya on the final evening of the retreat, I recognized infinity looking out first through his eyes and then my own. There was a spontaneous seeing that *I was* the infinite that I had experienced as a boy. I clearly was not who I thought I was! This recognition gradually unfolded more deeply into the body, especially the heart area, over a series of retreats until 2006, when there was no longer a natural movement to attend them. Since then, this deepening has continued on its own, penetrating into the core of the body.

As this inner knowing has grown in strength and clarity over the years, it has radiated out into all areas of my life, including my work with students and clients. As I was able to attune with this knowing in myself, I could sense and support its unfolding in others. I began to recognize the subtle somatic signs of this flame of inner knowing emerging in others. Whenever it did, people reported feeling more alive, real, connected, and empowered. As I recognized and mirrored this unfolding process of inner knowing back to them, it strengthened their recognition of this knowing within themselves, which, in turn, led them to be more self-confident and self-trusting. I discovered that once I began to point out these quiet bodily signs of inner knowing, people gradually began to recognize, trust, and act upon them by themselves. Their inner authority quickly grew.

Based upon my decades of close work with clients and students, I believe that anyone can get in touch with their inner knowing. The principles of sensing inner knowing and developing self-trust are universal. While an outer guide can be very helpful at times, these principles can be learned without a therapist, mentor, or teacher. This book will show you how. It is a mirror to help you recognize your own inner knowing by guiding you to carefully listen to your body.

Discovering Inner Resonance

Discovering inner resonance is my term for the process of learning to carefully listen to our body and recognize when it is telling us that we are resonating or attuning with our inner knowing. It comprises several steps.

The first step is to have an intellectual openness to the possibility that there are other ways of knowing than the rational mind. If we have a strong belief that inner knowing is a fantasy and that only analytic thought is trustworthy, we will not be open to listening to our body in a new way. It will be seen at best as a waste of time and at worst as self-delusive.

Take a minute and review your beliefs on the subject. Notice if there is some part of you that deeply doubts the possibility of an essential inner knowing. Make friends with it. Welcome it into awareness and get to know it better. At its core there may be some fear of being disappointed and hurt. An innocent trusting or early sensitivity may have been ridiculed or dismissed in a harsh family upbringing or school experience, exploited and distorted by an extreme religious doctrine, or badly burned in an intimate relationship.

In most cases, our doubt about an essential inner knowing is simply a matter of neglect. Our modern culture and education emphasize the value of rational, analytic thought, which is at the core of science and technology. Objective knowledge is verifiable, while subjective knowledge or wisdom apparently isn't. So inner knowing is left in the shadows, discarded as untrustworthy and without value. Yet objective knowledge without wisdom gives us many material possibilities with little real guidance about how to live in a way that is authentic, intimate, and deeply satisfying. It also leaves us with nuclear weapons and increasingly acute global warming and climate change. The rational mind is a good servant, but a poor master. It is important that it sees its limits and recognizes its rightful place as a useful tool. Our happiness and the planet's health depend on it.

If we are sufficiently open-minded, the next step is to begin to listen to our body. If we are willing and able to carefully listen, our body can sense when we are aligning with what is true for us. As we learn to recognize and understand the body's subtle sensations, and then act on them, our self-trust will grow tremendously. To me it is rather amazing that the body has this innate sense of the truth, as if the body is hardwired for it.

Listening to our body often means bringing our attention down and in—down from the forehead into the trunk of our body and its interior. Attention to the interior of the body is like sunshine and water for a plant—everything that it touches grows.

Using the following experiment, you can start right now by becoming acquainted with the heart area. You can create a recording of the script below, or you can have a friend read it for you. Whichever you choose, set aside fifteen minutes when you will not be disturbed. Turn off the ringer of your smartphone, close the door if needed, and find a comfortable place to sit upright in a relaxed way. Remind yourself that whatever needs doing can wait for a few minutes. Be sure to explore at a slow, comfortable pace.

EXPERIMENT *Listening to the Body*

Close your eyes and take a few deep breaths. Notice sounds in the environment, the weight of your body. Let yourself be held by whatever you are sitting on as well as the ground beneath you.

Notice where in your body your attention is localized. Often it is in the forehead. If so, gently redirect your attention to your chest. Imagine that your breath is directly entering and leaving the heart area.

Notice how the area of the heart feels. Does it feel open or closed, alive or numb, or something else? Take a minute or two and just sense what is here. As your attention rests here, you may notice subtle shifts of feeling or sensation. It's fine if your attention wanders off a bit; this is its nature. When you are aware that it has, gently bring it back to the heart area.

Now reflect on a specific time when you made a major life-changing decision that felt right. Perhaps it was committing to a partner or ending a relationship, choosing a new career, attending a school, or deciding to move. What do you notice in your body right now as you recall this decision? Take your time exploring the sensations.

Then focus on an important decision that you are currently making. As you sit with it, how does the heart area feel inside? How about the whole body? Is there a sense of peace and resonance, or is there some sense of discord? Simply take note without judgment.

As you come to the end, slowly open your eyes and reorient to your environment. Review your experience. You may want to make notes. ●

At first, consulting your body usually requires a certain degree of quiet and focus. In time it will become second nature. Attunement does not happen overnight. Just as it takes time to learn to play a musical instrument, it takes time and attention to listen deeply to the body's subtle guidance.

Sometimes when we are first learning to sense into our body, it may feel numb, chaotic, or emotionally painful. These sensations are examples of the static that needs to be cleared before we can hear the signal of inner knowing.

Once we feel a sense of inner resonance, it is important that we act on it. This completes and reinforces the process of discovering our inner knowing. If we fail to act on our inner knowing, it will recede into the background. Action reinforces our knowing and builds our self-trust. It also gives us very valuable feedback. If our inner knowing seems to be creating long-term suffering and discord for ourselves and others, it is very likely that we missed its signal the first time around. We need to test our inner knowing to be sure of its accuracy. This requires honesty and vulnerability.

Obstacles to Inner Knowing

Discerning a true sense of inner knowing can be a delicate task. There are many impostors. Most of what we call hunches or intuition is based upon fear or desire. Our inner knowing is heavily filtered by how we do or do not want things to be. When we have a strong attachment to an outcome, our sense of inner knowing is less clear. Our knowing is also deeply obscured by beliefs—what we believe about ourselves, others, and about life in general. For example, if we are convinced that we lack something essential or that the world is fundamentally hostile, we will miss the beauty and richness that life has to offer. In addition, reactive feelings of terror, rage, shame, and guilt are common forms of static that make it hard for most people to hear and decode the quiet signal of their inner knowing.

There are also dangers of inflation and grandiosity around apparent inner knowing. The mind wants to know so that it can plan and control what happens in order to keep the organism and the apparently separate self safe. Accordingly, it will grasp onto a false sense of knowing. This is particularly obvious with dictators and charismatic religious personalities, who are utterly convinced that their visions of reality are the only ones and who use their false certitude to inflict suffering upon others. The desire to be right is quite strong, and sometimes intuition or inner knowing can be used to justify our position as the only right one. New Age approaches that emphasize the power of the mind to create reality fall into this trap, promising that we can manifest whatever object we want by attuning with inner knowing. This is the arrogance of the mind.

While the process of getting in touch with your inner knowing is simple, it requires understanding, patience, and courage. It is a subtle art of deep listening that is infinitely rewarding.

Gifts of Inner Knowing

Recognizing and living in accord with our inner knowing does not guarantee an easy life or objectively successful outcomes. It does not ward off accidents (as we saw in Kelly's case), illness, or death. It does allow us to deal with these events with more inner space, grace, and creativity. Discovering and following the sense of inner knowing does not make us omniscient, rich, powerful, or famous, nor does it make us the master of the universe. If anything, it turns us into a humble servant of something that is unimaginably greater than our separate self. It does not put us in control of our life; it invites us to surrender what apparent control we have and to let go into a greater wisdom and a deeper love that is concerned with the whole of life.

Following our quiet inner knowing allows us to live more simply, freely, authentically, and intimately with life as it is. In a surprising way, it allows us to rest in not-knowing and to be more present where we actually are. As we rely increasingly on a quiet, body-based inner knowing, our thinking becomes secondary; it is dethroned as the CEO of our life and takes its rightful place as a useful assistant.

With inner knowing, we *feel* our way through life moment to moment with greater availability and creativity. Effective planning and analysis continue unburdened by obsessive self-concern and repetitive thought. We plan and then let go when there is nothing more to attend to. As the old religious saying suggests, we "do our best and let God do the rest." Yet this is no longer a prescription, but rather a description of how an inwardly attuned life functions. Insights tend to arise as needed, and the next obvious step makes itself known. If not, we simply wait for further guidance. It is the ending of drama and the beginning of a deeper life.

As we live in deeper accord with our own truth, we become more honest, open, and vulnerable. Our relationship with ourselves changes so that we are more intimate and accepting of our experience as it is. We come to see that any self-judgment creates distance from our experience and freezes it in place. We discover that whatever we resist persists.

As we are more authentic and intimate with ourselves, we become more authentic and intimate with others. Those relationships that were based on inauthenticity either evolve or fall away to be replaced by others that are more based in reality. This is often where the boat rocking that I mentioned earlier shows up most dramatically. We begin to discover what I call an *essential* way of relating, one that is not based on a bargained-for exchange that is the unconscious coin of orthodox relationships. I will say more about relationships in the final chapter; it is an important subject that often bewilders spiritual seekers who are looking for a transcendent peace.

Attuning with our inner knowing is an unfolding, open-ended, lifelong process. It doesn't end in some final, fully enlightened state. There is no finish line. Jean Klein described it as an ongoing crescendo. After many years of first seeking and then discovering, I find this a resonant description.

Getting Started

In this book I share insights, tell stories (please note that, with a few exceptions, clients' names are pseudonyms), and invite you to deeply inquire into your own direct experience.

The experiments throughout the book are opportunities to feel for yourself what inner knowing and inner resonance are all about.

Reading about inner knowing is good; experiencing your own inner knowing is even better. Some of the experiments are overlapping. I invite you to try them out—multiple times. I have used these inquiries and guided meditations in my groups, classes, workshops, retreats, and individual client sessions. They are potent.

In part 1, "Two Views of the Body," I review objective and subjective views of the phenomenon of attunement. In the first chapter, I explore the growing science of attunement and introduce you to attachment theory, mirror neurons, and interoception—the ability to sense into the interior of your body. Scientific research validates the critical role that attunement plays in healthy relationships and lets us know that there is more than imagination at work as we start to more carefully attune with ourselves and others. Learning of this research helps the skeptical mind to relax. In chapter 2, I discuss felt sensing, the subtle body, and the psycho-spiritual role of the seven major energy centers. Felt sensing is something that anyone can learn to do. Mapping the subtler energies of the body will help you to more quickly orient your inner listening.

It is hard to sense the body's subtle signals of inner knowing when our attention is absorbed in a reactive feeling, somatic contraction, and limiting belief. I think of these reactions as noise in the system. In part 2, "Reducing the Noise," I show how these reactions can become portals to our deeper knowing. We will focus on how to be with uncomfortable sensations and reactive feelings and how to question limiting beliefs, just as Kelly did.

Given the many obstacles and pitfalls to inner knowing, as well as its many impostors, how can we recognize and trust the real thing? While working intimately with people for many decades, I have identified four distinctive sensory markers that arise when we attune with our inner knowing: relaxed groundedness, inner alignment, open-heartedness, and spaciousness. Usually one or more of these qualities arises when we are in touch with our inner knowing. Part 3 explores each of these four bodily signals of inner knowing in depth.

In part 4, "The Fruits of Inner Knowing," I explore self-recognition and the great intimacy that unfolds from awakening to who we really are. This is what our inner knowing is drawing us toward.

Your inner knowing is quietly awaiting your attention. I invite you to slow down, sense into your body, and start listening in a new way. Trust your own direct experience and find out for yourself what it feels like to be in touch with *your* inner knowing. Discover how your life begins to move as you inwardly align. It is the most important experiment that you can do.

PART I

two views of the body

The body can be described in two ways: objectively and subjectively. Neuroscientists objectively describe the relationship between the brain, consciousness, and human relationships in order to better understand the phenomena of empathy and attunement. Subjectively, we can experience our body as a vibrant field of sensitivity capable of attuning to our inner experience or with others. These two views are complementary descriptions.

Our beliefs strongly filter our direct experience. As explorers, it is important that we use the best maps available. As we more clearly understand the innate sensitivity of the body and its highly refined capacity for attunement, we can approach our body with a more open mind. The more open-minded we are, the easier it will be to attune with our inner knowing.

the science of attunement

*The most beautiful thing we can
experience is the mysterious. It is the
source of all true art and science.*

ALBERT EINSTEIN

As David took a seat on my couch, he had a serious, intense look on his face. His long-term relationship was unraveling, and it looked like things were not going to end well. We quietly gazed with each other for a minute or two before he said, "I feel so unseen, unheard, and uncared for by her."

As I listened to him, I experienced a particular combination of feeling and sensation in the center of my chest. It was something very cold, dark, and icy—a place of deep pain in the heart area. When I shared this feeling with him, he tuned into his own body and responded, "Yes, it feels that way. There's a layer of rage here that I am reluctant to feel." He gestured toward his chest and continued, "Beneath that there is a terrible loneliness and feeling of isolation. This goes back a long time. I felt this way as a child."

As we continued to sit together, mostly in silence, and stayed with the difficult feelings and sensations, they began to thaw, like ice melting in the sun. After several minutes, David took a deep breath and said, "It feels warmer and lighter now. There is more of a sense of space and ease. I don't feel so alone with this." I also sensed that a shift had happened—the cold constriction in my heart area had passed.

Somehow I was sharing David's most difficult and intimate feelings without becoming lost in them. This spacious empathy, together with a shared focus of tenderness and understanding, allowed the feelings to transform by themselves. A three-way attunement was happening: David was attuning with his subtle interior feeling, I was attuning with mine, and we were attuning with each other. By attune, I mean to accurately sense and resonate with, as when a string on one guitar begins to vibrate in harmony with a string that has been plucked on another guitar.

What might contemporary science have to say about this attuned relational exchange? A surprising amount, it turns out.

Science is beginning to discover evidence for the kind of deeply subjective and attuned experiences that I shared with David. In this chapter we will take a quick tour through recent scientific research about attuning with others and ourselves, since the two are interrelated. I will touch upon the impact of a secure parent-child attachment on adult well-being, explore emotional resonance, describe the vital role that mirror neurons play in empathy, and touch upon our ability to attune with a deep, natural coherence within ourselves that corresponds to an inner knowing.

There may be a temptation to dismiss the relevance of any scientific investigation when we are exploring the sense of inner knowing that, by its nature, is self-validating. After all, we can usually sense to some degree when we are aligned and attuned with ourselves and when we are not. Yet we live in a scientific age, and empirical evidence is the currency of the time. The rational mind can relax more when it knows that intellectual honesty is at work and there is evidence supporting the existence of a sense of inner knowing. For some, objective evidence can calm the mind's doubt and encourage a more careful listening to the quiet inner voice of knowing.

At the same time, it is important to realize that our subtle inner experiences will never be fully defined by our scientific understanding. Correlation is not necessarily causation. Further, we are learning more every year about the transformative power of awareness, attention, and intention upon the mind and brain. At this point, I suspect we are only scratching the surface of how the brain, mind, and interpersonal relationships interact and influence the sense of inner knowing. When it comes to the study of consciousness, we are like the early Greek cartographers of the heavens; we are just beginning to explore this challenging and exciting field. This is especially true as we start to experience the separate sense of self softening and dissolving, and love, compassion, and wisdom flowering in its place.

Attachment Theory: How We Bond

Even though the spark of self-knowing lies deep within all of us, not all of us find it easy to trust and value ourselves. Having an attentive and attuned caretaker early in our lives helps enormously. We are multidimensional beings, and attunement can happen on multiple levels— physical, mental, emotional, and spiritual. Unless these levels are mirrored back to us in some way when we are young, it is harder for us to see and value them in ourselves as adults. Children need to *feel* that they are being seen, heard, and cared for. They need to *feel felt* by another.

When this early mirroring is highly distorted, it is as if we are continually viewing ourselves in one of those carnival fun-house mirrors. It is impossible to get an accurate sense of ourselves, much less trust ourselves. When we do receive sufficient attunement, the flame of self-trust and self-value naturally springs from a native ember and begins to blaze on its own. We are then better able to listen to and trust ourselves and navigate our lives with a growing degree of confidence and autonomy.

Infants are hardwired to connect with their caretakers. They are able to distinguish their mother's face and voice from others within thirty-six hours of birth. They also demonstrate a clear preference for and recognition of their mother's language early on, even when that language is spoken by others. This capacity for early mutual signal recognition has deep evolutionary roots. Bonding ensures survival. There is a remarkable scene in the 2005 documentary film *The March of the Penguins* that illustrates this. After months of being warmed and protected from the freezing Antarctic winter (mostly by the fathers, interestingly), penguin chicks hatch within a flock of thousands of adult birds, and both parents and chicks are able to recognize each other's voices within a deafening din of bird sound.

Babies need attuned attention—a caretaker who recognizes and actively responds to the baby's feelings and needs. The *quality* of the caretaker's attention is much more important than the *quantity* of time she or he spends with the baby. When normally responsive mothers face their one-year-old babies without showing any emotion on their faces, babies start to have an emotional meltdown within a minute as their attempts to elicit a response meet with failure. Babies look at faces so intently because they are tracking the feelings that our faces subtly express. Those wide-open eyes that are radiating baby *darshan* (a Sanskrit word referring to the benevolent radiance of a saint or sage) and the wonder of being are also looking for emotional attunement.

The mother's emotional responses need to be in sync with the baby's needs and feelings. Studies have shown that babies quickly become upset when viewing a prerecorded video of their mother's smiling face, yet the babies become content when they watch her face on a monitor where she can view and respond to her baby in real time. My wife and I have a delightful home video of our then four-month-old son experimenting with a series of coos and gurgles as my wife precisely mirrors back each sound. It is an amazing and very amusing duet! It also touches the heart in a deep way to witness such a beautiful and sonorous attunement.

Early emotional attunement and bonding have enormous con-sequences throughout our lives. As adults, we continue to enjoy and benefit from the fine-tuned mirroring of others, no matter how much we stand on our own. This is why having an empathically attuned friend, partner, or therapist can be valuable as we learn to attune to our inner knowing as adults. When we haven't received this type of attunement from our caretakers as children, we unknowingly crave it as adults and desperately search for it—usually in all the wrong places, as David did. We often pick partners who resemble our unavailable parent and try to win them over to prove our value to ourselves. Sadly, someone who is too available, too loving, just won't fill the bill. We don't value love unless it is hard won from an unavailable partner. Ultimately, no one else can completely fulfill us; self-love remains an inside job.

The field of psychotherapy has been strongly influenced in the past two decades by the growing body of research into what is called attachment theory—the study of how young children bond or fail to bond with their primary caretakers. These early ways of connecting and disconnecting with our parents have profound and pervasive effects upon our way of relating to others throughout our lives.

Building upon the earlier work of John Bowlby, MD, developmental psychologist Mary Ainsworth, PhD, initially described three types of childhood attachment styles: (1) secure, (2) ambivalent/resistant, and (3) avoidant.[1] A final style, disorganized, was added later.

A *secure* childhood attachment is linked with a parenting style that is prompt, appropriate, and consistent. Children raised this way experience their caretaker as a secure base from which they can explore the world. Parents who are inconsistently responsive generate insecure and *ambivalent* children, who are generally anxious and preoccupied with their caretaker's availability; these children both fear separation and warm slowly to reconnection. A child with an *avoidant* attachment style has been largely neglected by her primary caregiver and shows little feeling toward others. She has given up on connecting with others and feels low self-worth. Children frequently develop *disorganized* attachment styles when they have been mistreated and abused. They may try to soothe themselves by rocking their bodies or may become physically rigid or frozen in the face of danger.

You may want to take a little time right now to reflect on your experience of bonding when you were raised. Mary Main, PhD, a student of Ainsworth and a research psychologist at the University of California, Berkeley, developed the Adult Attachment Interview, which uses a series of open-ended questions to help parents assess their own experience of attachment as children.[2] Here is an abbreviated version offered by Daniel Siegel, MD, clinical professor of psychiatry at the UCLA School of Medicine.[3] Take a few minutes to ponder each of these inquiries and then take some notes.

Think of five words that reflect your earliest recollection of your childhood relationship with your mother.

Then think of an example for each word that illustrates a memory or experience that supports the word.

Now do the same exercise for your father, and for anyone else who was an attachment figure for you in your life (a grandparent, nanny, neighbor, older sibling).

Who were you closest to and why?

What was it like the first time you were separated from your parents or other caregivers?

What was it like for you, and for them, during this separation?

What would you do when you were upset?

If you were sick, injured, or emotionally distressed, what would happen?

Were you ever terrified of your caregivers?

How did your relationship with them change over the years?

Did anyone die during your childhood, or more recently?

Did anyone you were close to leave your life?

How were those losses for you, and how did they impact the family?

Are you close with your caregivers now?

Why do you think they acted as they did?

How did all of these things we've been exploring in
these questions influence your growth as an adult?

After considering these questions, what patterns do you detect in your
way of relating to others? Which of the four attachment styles seems
to best describe how you bond or resist bonding with others? Has your
style changed with self-knowledge and experience?

The four styles of attachment have been repeatedly tested and
verified using a method called "The Strange Situation," where one-
year-olds are carefully observed as they are exposed to parents and
strangers coming and going from a room during a twenty-minute
period. (Some of my clients experience their whole lives as "a strange
situation.") The results largely hold true across different cultures.
Each of these early childhood adaptive styles becomes a powerful
template and predictor for relationship styles in adolescence and
adulthood. The correspondence is not perfect, but these childhood
styles strongly influence how people relate to others as they grow
older. The meaning is clear: children who feel safe and attuned to
tend to thrive socially.

The research on attachment theory clearly shows how important
being attuned to by others is in attuning with ourselves. We first discover ourselves through the connection with and subtle mirroring of
others. When we are listened to, we learn to listen to ourselves. When
we are felt, we learn to recognize and value our feelings. When this
attunement is absent or lacking, we become a stranger to ourselves,
distant by degrees from our own direct experience. If our core needs
and feelings are ignored or devalued, we learn to suppress them. It
is simply too painful and unsettling to stay open. One result is that
we stop feeling and sensing the interior of our bodies. Our deeper
sensitivity is buried for safekeeping and then forgotten. This creates a
barrier to our inner knowing.

It is also important to recognize that no amount of secure attachment with a primary caretaker can address our existential anxiety as an apparent separate self who will become disabled and die. Only a deeply experiential inquiry into our true nature can address this fear. Our *most* secure base is revealed when we discover who we really are.

Emotional Resonance

The experience of *emotional resonance* is familiar to almost everyone. We can sometimes immediately sense what others are feeling, as if emotions are contagious. Great actors excel at evoking them; consider the exquisite artistry of Meryl Streep. The grief and joy of others can touch us deeply, sometimes overwhelmingly, and we can tell when someone is in a cheerful or depressed mood. I can often sense how my clients are doing before they say a word. How does this happen?

The Early Theory of Limbic Resonance

At the beginning of this century, three psychiatry professors at the University of California, San Francisco, Thomas Lewis, Fari Amini, and Richard Lannon, proposed the concept of *limbic resonance* in their popular and beautifully written book *The General Theory of Love* (2000) as a way to understand the deep emotional bonds that all mammals, especially humans, form.

They based their approach upon the triune brain model developed by the American neuroscientist Paul D. MacLean, MD, who in the 1960s proposed three distinct evolutionary layers of the brain: reptilian, limbic (paleomammalian), and neocortex.[4] According to MacLean, the middle or limbic brain governs emotions, which developed as a result of mammals giving birth to and caring for their babies, something reptiles never do. (Neuroscientists now consider the triune model of the brain to be oversimplified, despite its enduring popularity in the public mind. It turns out that the brain is not as discretely divided in either its form or its function as MacLean initially believed.)

According to the authors of *The General Theory of Love,* the limbic brain specializes in reading the inner states of other mammals and facilitating mutual attunement and a sense of communal connection. The limbic resonance between parent and child creates a *limbic regulation* in the child. Children cannot regulate their bodies or emotions for the first few years of their lives; instead, they rely on their parents for such regulation. Children's nervous systems and chemistry synchronize with those of their parents; for example, an infant's breathing and heart rate will entrain with her mother's when they sleep together. This limbic resonance with their parents teaches children to self-regulate physically and emotionally. If children do not receive the parental care needed to achieve limbic regulation, and thus do not learn how to regulate themselves, working with an empathic psychotherapist as an adult, regardless of his or her theoretical orientation, can create *limbic revision.*

Despite its popular appeal, the theory of limbic resonance has not generated much research or support in the scientific community since it was first proposed. While the theory was on the right track by accentuating the role of the limbic system in mediating emotional connections between people, it lacked precision and was quickly supplanted by the discovery of mirror neurons.

Mirror Neurons, Embodied Simulation, and Empathy

The adult brain weighs about three pounds and contains around one hundred billion neurons, or nerve cells. Neurons exist for the sake of all of the other cells in the body. They monitor internal states and interactions with the environment in order to maintain homeostasis, or balance. We experience our neurons' messages firsthand whenever we feel thirsty and cold. When we drink water or put on layers of clothing, we are responding to our neurons' signals to hydrate our cells or regulate our body temperature. According to Antonio Damasio, MD, PhD, a highly respected author, researcher, and professor of neuroscience at the University of Southern California, networks of neurons even mimic the body's structure and create an actual map of the body, a kind of "neural double."

The brain is able to map, transform, and, as we will see, simulate various body states.[5]

In the 1990s, researchers at the University of Parma in Italy were very surprised to discover that there were specific brain cells in macaque monkeys that could simulate the actions and intentions of other monkeys. Giacomo Rizzolatti and his team accidentally noticed that the same subtype of motor-control neurons fired whether a monkey ate a peanut or watched another monkey grasping and eating a peanut. In other words, what monkeys saw they also did in simulation. This phenomenon was completely unexpected, and it took a while for the incredulous researchers to recognize and understand the significance of what they had stumbled upon. The monkeys' brain cells were simulating, or mirroring, the experience of other monkeys as if they were having it themselves.[6]

These special nerve cells are now called *mirror neurons,* and they are believed to exist in far greater numbers and in much more highly developed networks in humans. The Italian researchers' findings may turn out to be revolutionary for the field of neuropsychology. V. S. Ramachandran, the eminent neurophysiologist and director of the Center for Brain and Cognition at the University of California, San Diego, says, "Mirror neurons will do for psychology what DNA did for biology."[7]

Why are they so important? The mirror-neuron system allows us to know in a visceral, firsthand way what others are planning to do, how they feel, and how they see the world. They allow us to effectively read one another's minds. This is extremely important for animals that live in groups—and humans are mammals that live cooperatively in groups par excellence. In order to safely and harmoniously live so closely together, we need to be able to quickly decode what others are experiencing. We need to immediately and accurately assess if someone is friend or foe, as well as navigate all of the subtle complexities of interacting and cooperating with one another. Just reflect upon how you feel when you enter into a new group of unfamiliar people. You may notice a subtle anxiety in yourself as you scan the group for a familiar face and wonder who you can safely approach.

Being able to *simulate* another's experience inwardly also allows us to *emulate* it outwardly. From birth, humans have an extraordinary ability to mimic the behavior of others. This miming ability, combined with the ability to vocalize, is the foundation for the development of language, which in turn allows for a very rapid transfer of learning between generations. Ramachandran hypothesizes that humans' development of tools, fire, shelter, language, and a theory of mind (imagining another's intentions, perspectives, and feelings) may have come about due to the rapid development of mirror neurons somewhere between 75,000 and 100,000 years ago. Human evolution went into hyperdrive as knowledge was transferred via culture rather than the excruciatingly slow and inefficient process of natural selection. Ramachandran suggests that by "hyper-developing the mirror-neuron system, evolution turned culture into the new genome."[8]

Mirror neurons allow humans to empathize with one another. Vittorio Gallese, MD, a member of the original team of University of Parma researchers and a professor of physiology, has formulated the theory of embodied simulation to account for empathy.[9] Whereas other theories of empathy rely on a self-reflective process of comparing our own experience with that of another in order to get a sense of what the other may be experiencing, Gallese and others argue that empathy is largely mediated by the mirror-neuron system; it is primarily pre-reflective and directly experienced in our body prior to any cognitive process. Various types of mirror neurons allow us to directly experience what others are doing, intending to do, and, most importantly, feeling—both physically and emotionally.

Facial expressions are a key way of signaling feelings. Paul Ekman, PhD, a longtime professor and researcher (now retired) at the University of California, San Francisco, discovered that human emotions and their facial expressions are consistent in populations across cultures, from American grad students to preliterate Papua New Guineans.[10] Mirror neurons allow us to simulate the facial expressions of others and then transfer this information through the insular cortex (part of the cerebral cortex that is linked with emotions, consciousness, and homeostatic regulation) to the limbic system, which largely governs our emotions. Because mirror neurons are also sensitive to sound and context, we are able to receive and decode very nuanced emotional messages from others. We can then feel what others are feeling with a high degree of accuracy; we can both discern and accurately simulate someone else's emotional experience *within our own body*.

We can also sense what others are sensing. Ramachandran calls some of these mirror neurons (the anterior cingulate pain sensory neurons) "Gandhi neurons" because they allow us to directly feel the physical pain of others. Ramachandran is famous for his work with the phenomenon of phantom limb pain, in which he demonstrated that the brain continues to simulate the existence of a limb even after it has been lost. Some patients who have lost an arm, for instance, complain of pain in their missing limb for months after an accident or amputation. How does one alleviate pain in an arm that doesn't exist? There was no solution until Ramachandran discovered a very simple and clever way to do so: when patients sit in front of a mirror that reflects an image of their remaining arm in the place of their missing arm, they feel as if their missing arm has been restored. Moving the remaining arm, which is reflected in the mirror, alleviates the pain in the phantom arm. Patients experience the immediate relief of pain through this virtual massage.

Even more surprising, when a person with a missing or anesthetized arm watches another person being administered a shot in the equivalent arm, they feel it as acutely as if it were happening directly to them. These so-called Gandhi neurons cannot distinguish between self and other. One might be tempted to say that they function in a nondual way, where the apparent distinction between subject and object dissolves. Without the experience of the boundary of our skin, we experience everything as if it were happening to our own body. Ramachandran writes, "Imagine: the only thing separating your consciousness from another's might be your skin!"[11]

While this undifferentiated experience can sound like a very developed mystical state, in practice it is very confusing. It is impossible to function as an organism if we cannot distinguish our body from someone else's. In fact, this state usually doesn't happen because other areas of the brain dampen or nullify the input from the pain sensory neurons. Nature has worked out a balance so that we usually get enough of the other's experience to empathize without becoming lost in their pain. Too much empathy is paralyzing.

Marco Iacoboni, MD, PhD, a researcher at UCLA's Brain Research Institute, believes that mirror neurons "were selected because they provide the adaptive advantage of intersubjectivity."[12] Those humans who could "read the minds" and cooperate with others had a better chance of surviving. Mirror neurons have enhanced the human species' ability to survive by allowing us to decode others' intentions and feelings so that we can get along with one another. The implications are enormous. Iacoboni suggests that evolution is actually selecting mirror neurons for empathy rather than individual selfishness, for interdependence rather than independence. He also suggests that the strict demarcation between self and other is deeply mistaken and that it is important for us as a society to question our long-standing beliefs, particularly in the West, about our separate individuality. The discovery of mirror neurons makes explicit what has been implicit all along: we are unimaginably interconnected.

Beyond the Mirror Neurons

Our fundamental interconnectivity and capacity for mutual attunement or resonance is almost certainly mediated by additional mechanisms of which we are unaware. I strongly suspect that mirror neurons only partially explain the ways that we can intimately sense one another. We sometimes experience finer, energetic levels of connection—levels that are beyond the level of observable actions and feelings. These connections seem to have much more to do with sensing via the heart or the gut than the brain.

Late one night years ago, when I was researching my doctoral dissertation, I read a book by a man in Jungian analysis who kept a journal of his dreams as he approached his impending death from cancer. In one of his dreams, everyone he had ever been close to came to him at his deathbed, where he forgave them or asked them for their forgiveness.

I was deeply touched by the man's description of his dream. I decided to lie down on my bed, imagine that I was dying, and then see who would spontaneously appear so that I might end my life with a sense of completion with them. At one point, a very close friend from high school appeared. He and I had had a falling out five years before over our separate spiritual paths. At the time, I had felt that he had betrayed my trust, and I had cut off all further contact with him. As I opened to his presence that evening, I suddenly realized that he had also felt betrayed by me. My heart opened, and inwardly I sincerely forgave him and asked him to forgive me.

Two days later, he called me at work, having gotten my number from my mother. He reported that the day before, he had been driving down the freeway and began to cry so hard while thinking of me that he had to pull over. We soon reconciled, and he became one of the groomsmen at my wedding later that year.

I doubt that mirror neurons, at least as we currently understand them, can explain this kind of deep, heartfelt connection.

What Is the Self That We Are Attuning With?

In a way, it is much easier to talk about attuning with others than about self-attunement. At least we can see and hear the other. But what is this self with which we attune? As we will see, it is (we are) quite a mysterious subject—pun intended.

Antonio Damasio suggests that the self is like the conductor of a symphony, but with an unusual twist: the symphony (brain activity) creates the conductor. This does not mean that the self is unreal, he writes, only that it exists within the mind. According to Damasio, in order to have consciousness we need: "(1) [to] be awake; (2) to have an operational mind; and (3) to have, within that mind, an automatic, unprompted, undeduced sense of self as protagonist of the experience, no matter how subtle that sense may be." He goes on to identify two kinds of consciousness, core and autobiographical:

> The minimal-scope kind I call **core** consciousness,
> the sense of the here and now, unencumbered by

much past and by little or no future. It revolves
around a core self and is about personhood but not
necessarily identity. The big-scope kind I call extended
or **autobiographical** consciousness, given that it
manifests itself most powerfully when a substantial
part of one's life comes into play and both the
lived past and the anticipated future dominate the
proceedings. It is about personhood and identity.[13]

The core self is a composite of feelings of knowing (I am the knower),
object saliency (what makes something stand out from other things),
perspective (I am in here), ownership (this body is mine), and agency
(I am doing it).

Ramachandran writes that the conscious self neither "inhabits a
special throne at the center of the neural labyrinth," nor is it a "prop-
erty of the whole brain. Instead, the self seems to emerge from a
relatively small cluster of brain areas that are linked into an amazingly
powerful network."[14]

Thomas Metzinger, PhD, an influential philosopher of consciousness at the Johannes Gutenberg University in Mainz, Germany,
taking a slightly different angle, argues that there is no self as such,
but rather only a *phenomenal self model* that is a process rather than
a thing.[15] According to Metzinger, this "transparent" or invisible self
model exists within a world model and provides a first-person perspective—what we experience as subjectivity. He calls this an ego tunnel.
Even though we have a robust experience of the reality of the self and
the world—what is known as naïve realism—both are virtual con-
structs, a representation of reality rather than reality itself.

For instance, what we experience as our body is actually a model
or simulation in our brain. This is beautifully demonstrated with the
rubber-hand illusion. If you happen to have a rubber or plastic hand
or foot lying around, you can try the following experiment. You can
also view it on YouTube. The experiment requires two people, the
subject and the researcher. The subject extends both arms out in front
of herself on a table; however, one of her arms is placed slightly to the

side and partially shielded from her view by a barrier. The researcher places a detached, lifelike rubber hand in the place where the subject's real hand would normally be resting. He then takes two small, soft brushes and simultaneously strokes both the subject's hidden hand and the rubber hand in the same place for a minute or two. In a little while, most subjects feel that the rubber hand is theirs. Further, they will react nervously if the rubber fingers are bent into contorted positions or if the fake hand is suddenly stabbed with a pencil. The virtual body image has been stimulated visually and tactilely, and an illusion is experienced as being real. The brain fills in the gap and claims the rubber hand as its own.

After first reading about this experiment, I managed to find a pair of plastic feet that my wife had used for studying reflexology years before and gave the experiment a try. The plastic feet were about three-quarters life size and had clearly visible markings, with the names of various organs and body parts, such as "breast" and "diaphragm," written and encircled on the surface. There were even Chinese characters visible on top of the stump. Even though the plastic foot looked significantly different from a true human foot, my brain mistook the false foot as its own. Within seconds of the toes being brushed, the plastic foot began to feel as if it was mine.

I became curious to see what would happen if I replaced my wife's real hand with a plastic foot. Barely able to suppress my laughter, I shielded her right arm from her view and placed a plastic foot on a table in her line of vision and began brushing it. Sure enough, she reported feeling as if it were her own hand. I had the same experience. In addition to being a fabulous party trick, this experiment demonstrates how intrinsic and malleable our body image is.

Because the sense of being in a body (perspective), owning a body (ownership), and operating a body (agency) are such fundamental parts of self-identity, Metzinger was interested in the phenomenon of out-of-body experiences (OBEs), a few of which he had experienced as a young man. He knew that this experience could be induced in part by stimulating a particular area of the brain (the right angular gyrus) and was curious whether the rubber-hand illusion could be extended to include the whole body by using virtual technology. First he used a head-mounted display that created the illusion of a 3-D room in front of him. Next, using a camera mounted behind him, he videotaped the image of his back being stroked. Finally, he projected the videotaped image of his back in front of himself, with the help of a 3-D encoder, and watched this image in the head-mounted display. He reported feeling as if he was being partially drawn into the virtual body before him.

Metzinger has found no convincing evidence that people who report OBEs actually leave their bodies and travel elsewhere. He suspects that the subjective experience of being out of the body is the source of the widespread cultural belief that there is an incorporeal soul that is distinct from the body and survives physical death. For Metzinger, the "subtle body" exists only as "pure information flowing in the brain."

Despite Metzinger's skepticism on the matter, anecdotal evidence suggests that OBEs may sometimes be more than purely subjective phenomena. According to Sam Parnia, MD, PhD, a critical care physician and director of resuscitation research at the Stony Brook University School of Medicine in New York, a revolution in resuscitative medicine is allowing some people to come back to life from several minutes to hours after their heart, breath, and brain activity have ceased—the normal definition of death. And there have been some apparently accurate reports of "dead" people hearing and seeing events that that they couldn't have experienced unless some part of them left their physical bodies.[16] The issue of the subtle body in general is an important thread that runs throughout this book and one that I will explore much more fully in the next chapter. Genuine OBEs may be one expression of the subtle body.

I think it is safe to say that much of what we experience as our self is a product of brain functioning. Yet there are compelling anecdotal accounts of a rich, coherent subjectivity that endures even when neocortical activity is deeply compromised by coma or when people temporarily meet the ordinary criteria for being dead. While we can more or less consciously attune with different dimensions of our experience—physical, emotional, and mental—who we ultimately are remains an open mystery.

Interoception: Sensing Inside the Body

An important part of self-attunement is being able to sense and feel what is going on in the interior of our body, whether we think the body is virtual or real. Physiologists call this type of sensing *interoception*. Most of us unknowingly live above the neck, lost in our thoughts. Psychotherapists often help their clients get in touch with their bodies as a way to become more intimate with their experience and to be more in touch with themselves and others. As we saw at the beginning of this chapter, my client David's ability to sense into the emotional pain and contraction in the heart area, and my ability to attune with him, allowed for a significant shift in his inner feeling state. Being able to sense into our bodies, particularly the chest and belly, is a critical step in self-attunement and attunement with others.

In his book *The Mindful Therapist*, Daniel Siegel writes:

> Interoception is the skill of perceiving the interior of our
> body. As we . . . focus a spotlight of attention on this internal
> world of our bodily states, we draw upon the sensations of
> our muscles, the signals from our heart and intestines, the
> overall feeling inside of ourselves. Interoception is a crucial
> aspect of the monitoring function of the mind that opens
> the gateway to attunement with others.[17]

While I was sitting with David, I could sense an icy feeling in my chest area that I suspected was in some way resonant with his inner experience. I am no longer surprised when these kinds of sensations are resonant; however, I don't assume that my feelings and sensations always accurately match those of my client. Our own conditioning can get activated and strongly filter or distort our attunement with others. While we can get a lot of useful information from our hearts and guts, the process is not foolproof. Siegel notes, "Our gut feelings are in no way always accurate, but they often provide an important source of knowing." This ability to sense into the interior of our body, to *interoperceive*, is directly related to *felt sensing,* a term coined in the early 1960s by the pioneering philosopher and psychotherapist Eugene Gendlin, PhD.

We will explore this phenomenon of the felt sense more fully in the next chapter.

Resonance and the Sense of Inner Knowing

No researcher has contributed more to the scientific conversation about attunement and resonance than Daniel Siegel, co-director of the Mindful Awareness Research Center and professor of psychiatry at UCLA, who founded the interdisciplinary approach of Interpersonal Neurobiology in 1999. Siegel is fearless in discussing issues such as presence, resonance, intuition, wholeness, and truth, which most neuroscientists carefully avoid. His wide-ranging, integrative perspective has particular relevance to the subject of this book.

Siegel distinguishes between attunement and resonance. Attunement can be with oneself (*intra*personally) or with another (*inter*personally). Resonance refers to mutual attunement, where there is an entrainment between two (or more) people and where each person is transformed as she or he takes in the internal state of the other. When the people in question hold a respect and regard for one another, Siegel notes, "a deep feeling of coherence emerges with the subjective sensation of harmony."[18] This is a beautiful description of what happens in any kind of truly intimate meeting between people. There is something profoundly touching and nurturing that we feel when this happens.

This kind of deep resonance evokes a feeling of wholeness with no loss of one's individuality. In an experience that can be puzzling to the mind, we retain the sense of being a unique individual as we also sense our profound connectedness. When this resonance happens at the deepest level, we can sense our nonseparate nature: we are neither one nor two. In a particularly lyrical passage of *The Mindful Therapist*, Siegel writes:

> Attuning to others, we open ourselves to the profound
> adventure of linking two as part of one interactive whole.
> This joining is an intimate communion of the essence
> of who we are as individuals yet truly interconnected

with one another. It is hard to put into words, but
resonance reveals the deep reality that we are a part of
a larger whole, that we need one another, and, in some
ways, that we are created by the ongoing dance within,
between, and among us.[19]

Siegel's work is all about integration—the linkage of differentiated
parts. An integrated system is flexible, adaptive, coherent, energized,
and stable. (Siegel, who seems to love acronyms, calls these qualities
the FACES of integration.) The quality of integrated coherence refers
to truth. He is talking about the way things from the past fit together
and make sense to us, fostering a present-centered authenticity and
an ability to accurately predict the future. Truth and integration are
mutually supportive.

I often see this integrative process in my work with clients when
they open to their experience as it is. As my clients honestly feel their
sometimes difficult feelings and sensations and are able to link them to
their origins, their lives start making sense. A coherent narrative emerges,
along with a feeling of growing inner and outer harmony and connection. When this narrative is held lightly and, in a certain way, seen
through, an even more profound sense of wholeness becomes available.

Interestingly, this sense of coherence appears to have neurological
correlates. Antoine Lutz, PhD, an associate scientist at the Waisman
Lab for Brain Imaging and Behavior at the University of Wisconsin–
Madison, discovered that eight long-term practitioners of a type of
Tibetan unconditional loving-kindness and compassion meditation
generated a very specific kind of brain-wave synchrony, where neurons oscillated at the same high frequency across different sections
of the brain (a.k.a. neural synchrony). Both novice and experienced
meditators were instructed to "let their mind be invaded by a feeling
of love or compassion . . . toward all sentient beings without thinking
specifically about anyone in particular." The highly experienced meditators were able to generate extraordinary levels of neuronal synchrony
or coherence.[20] Other kinds of brain-wave synchrony have also been
observed with experienced Transcendental Meditation practitioners.[21]

When experienced meditators tune in to loving-kindness or silence, their brain waves become more coherent. These objective measurements of coherence correlate with meditators' subjective reports of feeling deeply attuned. When we are in touch with our inner knowing, we also feel inwardly attuned; there is a sense of things coming together and lining up inside. We feel more whole and coherent. While we don't need to measure our brain waves to sense when we are in touch with our inner knowing, it is interesting to see that there are measurable effects in our brain when we are deeply attuned with ourselves.

Rick Hanson, PhD, neuropsychologist and author of *Buddha's Brain* and *Hardwiring Happiness*, has highlighted how the brain's negative bias toward potential survival threats can be gradually retrained toward letting in positive experiences through purposeful attention. Mindfulness—focused attention—is one of the key tools that can take advantage of the brain's neuroplasticity and shift subjective experience toward happiness. He writes, "People who have practiced deeply in the contemplative traditions are the 'Olympic athletes' of the mind. Learning how they've trained their minds (and thus their brains) reveals powerful ways to have more happiness, love, and wisdom."[22]

One of the most rigorous and comprehensive studies of meditation to date is the Shamatha Project. In it, sixty experienced meditators were randomly assigned either to a three-month intensive meditation retreat led by Buddhist scholar and teacher Alan Wallace or to a control group. Participants underwent various lab assessments and filled out questionnaires before, during, and after the study. Results showed that "intensive contemplative training sharpens and sustains attention, enhances well-being, and leads to less judgmental, more empathic emotional responding to the suffering of others. Additionally, the training was linked with pro-social emotional behavior and important physiological markers of health."[23]

What is at the very heart of these contemplative practices? Siegel describes a ground of being in the very center or hub of the mind that is different from the content of awareness. "To know and cultivate the truth," he writes, "we need to differentiate what we are aware of from the experience of awareness." In his model, as we learn to be aware of various outer and inner sensations, along with thoughts and images, we may also notice a very subtle "perception of our deep interconnected nature. The boundaries of 'you' and of 'me' become permeable, the steep walls between us come down, and the notion of a wholly separate self begins to dissolve."[24]

Siegel is clearly writing from his own direct experience—one that also has been reported by a number of my clients and colleagues. Give it a try right now for ten minutes.

EXPERIMENT   *Can You Locate Awareness?*

Take a minute to close your eyes, and take a few deep breaths and relax.

Notice the sensations of touch, sound, taste, and smell. Notice any sensations inside your body. Be aware of any feelings that you are experiencing.

Now note your thoughts. Don't try to think or to not think; just be aware of the comings and goings of thoughts and images, usually of the past or the imagined future.

Now turn your attention to this which is aware—aware of sensations, feelings, and thoughts. Does it have a discrete location or boundary? Is it possible that this open, undefined awareness is shared by everyone? ●

Siegel describes *knowing* as "a nonconceptual inner sense of truth, an intuitive and non-language-based way of perceiving the nature of reality and our place in the larger world and the continuity within the flow of life in which we live." This form of knowing is an unworded way of coming to the truth, a subterranean stream that provides "a coherent impression of the world as it is."

> We bring the "wisdom of the body" up into our cortical
> consciousness. But the sense of this wisdom is not
> a logical thought or even a constructed conceptual
> category. The wave of information, perhaps flowing

from the parallel-distributed processors of the intestines
(a gut feeling) and the heart (a heartfelt sense) as well as
from the integrative circuits throughout the brain may
give us a deep sense of nonconceptual knowing.[25]

Using the language of neuroscience, Siegel is directly pointing to the
central theme of this book: the sense of inner knowing. Significantly,
he links it to the wisdom of the body, a subject that we will explore
through direct experience in the next chapter.

Summary

Scientific research is validating the critically important role that attunement with ourselves and others plays in fostering a sense of well-being.
Decades of research on attachment theory demonstrate that early parent-
child bonding strongly influences how we connect with others as adults
and also shapes how well we attend to and value our own needs and
feelings. When we are listened to early on, we are more likely to listen
to ourselves as adults. Inner listening allows access to our inner knowing.

We are also discovering some of the neurological components
of emotional attunement or resonance with others. Mirror neurons—"monkey see, monkey do" brain cells—are able to simulate the
actions of others, allowing us to accurately feel their feelings, sense
their sensations, and understand their intentions within our own body.
Mirror neurons allow us to empathize via an embodied simulation,
which fosters cooperation and the survival of the species. Evolution
appears to be supporting this movement toward greater interpersonal
attunement and empathy.

Most neuroscientists believe that our sense of subjectivity is purely
a brain construct. Experiments like the rubber-hand illusion demonstrate how we experience the brain's simulation of the body as if it is
real. Experiences of the subtle body may only be in the brain; however,
richly coherent anecdotal accounts from people who have returned
from clinically defined death or near-death caution us to keep an open
mind on the subject.

One of the practical ways that we are able to attune with our inner experience is through interoception—the ability to sense into the interior of our body. This objective capacity closely corresponds with subjective experience of felt sensing.

Daniel Siegel has done pioneering research into the phenomenon of attunement and interpersonal resonance. He links the sense of inner knowing and truth with the quality of coherence, one of the facets of an integrative system. Researchers have discovered that long-term meditators exhibit different kinds of brain-wave coherence, in addition to sharper attention and greater empathy. When we are deeply attuned with ourselves, sensing a profound silence or feeling very openhearted, we can directly experience this sense of inner coherence.

2

felt sensing and the subtle body

The body is your nearest environment.
JEAN KLEIN

Corinne was wrestling within herself. She needed to make enough money to help support her family, yet the work that she most wanted to do—helping children who have been exposed to sexual abuse—paid much less than her current job. It would also require her to spend less time with her own children. She felt torn; she wanted to be true to herself and also be a responsible parent. What was the right thing to do? Her mind couldn't figure it out.

I also didn't know what was right for her, though I had a hunch, based upon a feeling of vibrancy that I sensed in my heart area whenever she mentioned helping abused children.

I encouraged Corinne to slow down and to feel her body. She took a breath, and her attention dropped down to her heart area and belly. The crease in her brow relaxed as she quietly listened to her body-based inner knowing.

After a minute of silence, she looked up and said, "You know, if I do what I really love, I will be a better parent to my children. I may not be around quite as much, but I will be a lot happier when I am. I don't know how I will make this work financially, but it feels right to me. It feels like my life's work."

As Corinne quietly listened to her body, she discovered an unexpected clarity that her ordinary thinking mind could not find. When she shared her insight, it resonated for both of us. It rang true inside in a way that was palpable. Her direction was clear, even if the steps to make it happen were not. Her attention dove into the interior of her body, and she emerged with an important pearl of self-understanding.

The inside of our body is a terra incognita for many of us. What is your sense of it right now? At first it may be hard to describe this vague landscape in words. A different vocabulary, one of images and metaphors, is often better suited for the job. Sometimes when clients come into my office and comment on the weather, I will ask them for an "inner weather report," too. Is it crisp and sunny inside, or perhaps overcast, damp, and foggy? Is there a storm brewing on the horizon? We all have the capacity to be an accurate inner meteorologist, although it generally takes some time and attention to become good at it. Most importantly, we need to be willing to find out what is actually going on.

Some people are naturals at this. They know how to slow down, feel into the interior of their bodies, and begin to find words and images that resonate with what they subtly sense. They are able to be in touch with themselves and how their lives are unfolding. These folks also tend to benefit the most from psychotherapy regardless of the therapist or the therapist's theoretical framework. This important discovery was made by the philosopher and psychotherapist Eugene Gendlin, PhD, who spent fifteen years at the University of Chicago with the preeminent American psychologist Carl Rogers, PhD, researching factors that led to effective psychotherapy.

Gendlin discovered that certain clients had the native ability to tune in to their inner experience and get a sense of what was going on. They always received the most benefit from psychotherapy. This outcome could be accurately predicted within the first two sessions. In 1963, Gendlin coined the phrase "felt sense" to describe this phenomenon. He found that there is a kind of internal body awareness that, although used occasionally by only a few people, could be learned by anyone. This discovery is one of the most insightful and useful to come out of twentieth-century psychotherapy. It has both transformed and transcended its own field, since anyone can learn and practice it on their own. Its applications go far beyond psychotherapy.

The Far Reach of Felt Sensing

According to Gendlin, the felt sense is the preverbal, whole-body sense of something that is vague and unknown at first; it arises from the "body *and* mind before they are split apart." It may be related to a current problem, something nagging from the past, an insight, an unfolding situation, or anything else. In a 1981 interview, Gendlin said:

> What is not yet clear can be directly sensed in the body. And there is a special level, a special kind of space, a special kind of attention that most people don't know, to allow the body to form a wholistic sense of some problem. . . . *It includes everything one knows* [italics added], but it is always a single whole, a single sense.[1]

Once a felt sense comes into awareness and is sufficiently explored, something very interesting occurs. Gendlin describes a distinctive felt shift that happens, a shift accompanied by a "coming unstuck" and "a relief and a coming alive"—key components of a transformative insight. His description matches that of one of the markers of inner knowing that I will explore in chapter 5: relaxed groundedness. The sense of coming alive is often intimately linked with the sense of inner alignment, another marker of inner knowing (see chapter 6). He observed that we can sense when something is genuinely open or resolved within us and when something new emerges that feels both natural and good. Based on observations of his naturally gifted clients, Gendlin gradually developed research-based guidelines to help anyone discover felt sensing. He called his method *focusing*. He acknowledges that some people will learn it more quickly than others. There are six steps to the classic focusing protocol:

1. Clearing a space

2. Getting a felt sense

3. Getting a handle

4. Resonating

5. Asking

6. Receiving

Interest in focusing within the professional psychotherapy community, as well as among the public, continues to be robust more than fifty years after Gendlin's groundbreaking discovery of the felt sense. I originally trained in focusing when I was a graduate student in 1980. It made immediate sense to me at the time, and I continue to informally use some of its principles and practices, particularly felt sensing and checking for resonance.

Over time I have been surprised to discover the far reach of felt sensing. The body's natural capacity to holistically sense goes far beyond its ability to sense a specific problem or situation. It includes perceiving the very subtle energies that are described in some Eastern contemplative traditions, which I will discuss shortly, as well as sensing our deepest self.

Our bodies are extraordinarily sensitive instruments that respond to inner and outer environments with remarkable accuracy when they are not cluttered with the static of mental and emotional confusion. We can have a felt sense of another person, a situation that we are in, or an internal state, as my client Corinne did; this is what Gendlin was initially tracking with his research into effective psychotherapy. Yet we can also sense into our connection with the whole of life. Not only is the body embedded in the emergent flow of life, but it also is an expression of this flow and has a sense of the source of this flow. Like the game where a group of children yell "warm, warmer, hot" as someone gets closer to a hidden object, the body has a native sense of what is deeply true or real. The far reach of felt sensing can help lead us to knowing who we really are.

The far reach of felt sensing embraces everything, including our sense of knowing. Often this felt sense of wholeness involves the areas of the heart and belly, the same regions that Daniel Siegel identified with the ability to interoperceive (see chapter 1). Felt sensing and interoperceiving appear to be describing very similar functions—subjective and objective sides of the same coin. Each refers to a subtle ability that allows for the direct and intuitive sensing of our deepest truth.

Candice's Inner Oracle

Candice tended her beautiful garden and wide network of friends and family with equally deep care. She was gradually learning to include herself in this caring embrace. She was one of those naturals at felt sensing, but instead of "felt sensing" she called it "listening to my oracle." It was easy to see why. Once she settled into our sessions, with her dream journal and water bottle close at hand, she would offer a casual internal weather report, sometimes with sighs and often with self-amused, vibrant laughter. Then, as she would start to listen more carefully to herself, unexpected images, intuitive connections, and deeper questions would arise.

Today she wondered out loud about the purpose of her life, with all of its frequent errands and busyness. I invited her to slow down and sit with her question, which she did for a minute in silence.

"Hmm," she said with a note of surprise. Her pace of speech and thought slowed, and the flow of images and body sensations began to emerge. I felt like I was sitting next to a sparkling stream in the High Sierras. The oracle was coming online.

Here is her description:

> And softly, the images begin to flow—quiet poetic
> images. I see my heart. It has been pierced by a huge
> sword. I feel that this is my past, the suffering. But now,

I am told, I'm here to soften the heart. But the heart
is the threshold to all that I want—peace, harmony,
knowing all things to be radiant. The heart must be
allowed to soften, thence to shine.

I pull the sword out of my heart—I feel like King
Arthur pulling out the sword in the stone. I know that
I hold knowledge in my hand, that the portal to the
essence of my being has been suffering, the pierced heart.
But now, to allow the true heart to shine and be radiant,
the heart only needs to soften.

Then the heart glows. It's all I need. I say, "I don't
know why I, of all people, did not know that the
small gesture is huge." There is not so much I have
to do. Access to the core of being is in the smallest
gesture—the sitting down, the breath.

Candice gently laid her hand on her heart area. "It is not about *doing*
anything great or special," she said. "My life can be very ordinary. In
fact, it is *how* I live it. Can I fully accept my life just as it is?"

She stopped to briefly ponder the question.

"Now that would be extraordinary!" she said, with a note of awe
in her voice. And then, after another pause, she added, "You know,
the only teaching I need, the one I keep next to my bed, is this one
[from Adyashanti]: 'The spiritual task we are given is a simple one:
to attend to that inner spark of radiance, to hold vigil over it until we
realize it to be our self, and to dig up and cast off all argument we have
with its love.'"

The Head and the Heart

Much of what we call the spiritual journey involves a shift of attention
from the head to the heart. Although they are only a short distance from
each other, they are worlds apart in terms of experiencing life. It was no
mistake that Candice initially gestured with her hands around her head
as she described her sense of busyness. Nor was it mere coincidence

when she rested her hand over the center of her chest as she tapped into her inner oracle—the upwelling spring of intuitive knowing. When she let in the insight that her life did not need to be extraordinary or special in order to have purpose—that it becomes deeply meaningful when she fully accepts it as it is—I sensed a further relaxing and grounding in her as her inner center of gravity dropped down to another level. Within a few minutes, Candice's attention had traversed the inner landscape of head, heart, and belly (*hara*).

EXPERIMENT *Where Does Your Attention Center?*

Close your eyes, take a few deep breaths, and turn your attention to the interior of your body. Without trying to change anything, notice where your attention is seated. Where does it center? Is it in the forehead? This is the most common home for those of us who rely a lot on our thinking. Is it in the heart area—the center of feeling? Or perhaps is it lower down, in the belly? Become acquainted with a sense of this localized attention. •

We live in our heads when we are lost in our thoughts. It is easy to do. To live in our head means that attention is largely centered in the forehead—what Jean Klein, one of my main teachers, playfully calls "the factory of thought." We can sense it in ourselves and others. "They are in their head," we will sometimes say when we encounter people who are dryly mental, abstract, and not in touch with their feelings or their bodies. It can happen to us when we spend too much time looking at a screen, anxiously ruminating, or engaging in a superficial conversation. When this happens for me, there is an uncomfortable sensation of heat in the forehead that brings to mind the image of an overheated car engine. It is a signal for me to pull over and take a break from whatever it is that I am doing.

Thinking in itself is not the problem. We often need to think—the clearer, the better. The problem arises when we believe our thoughts and *identify* with our thinking. We let our thoughts define and confine us and, by extension, everyone and everything else. When we believe

our judgmental thoughts, we are in prison. When we confuse thinking with reality, we suffer. We then radiate our suffering out to others.

While some thoughts are more accurate than others, none are ultimately true; they are symbolic representations of our experience. When
we begin to realize that awareness is distinct from thought, attention
becomes more spacious and free. I will cover this critically important
subject much more thoroughly in chapter 4.

As we learn to see our thoughts *as thoughts* instead of reality, attention naturally drops down from the forehead into the heart area. This
is usually a slow, gradual process of reorientation, although there can
be many initial forays of attention into the heart along the way. It can
take us a while to find our way and create a new path. Whenever attention shifts from the head to the heart, the heart becomes increasingly
familiar and less foreign. In time, we sense it as our new home.

The heart area is, above all, the center of deep feeling and sensitivity. When the heart area is illumined, we have a vibrant sense of
the wholeness of life. What thought divides, the heart unites. Our
argument with reality ends when our attention is deeply seated in
the heart. It's not that we become passively resigned. Instead, we
first accept things as they are and then become available to respond
creatively. On occasion, the response may be quite fierce and force-
ful, but it will not carry the residues of personal insult, shame, or
self-righteous anger. Every situation contains a solution. When our
attention rests in the heart, we feel our way to the solution with
much greater grace and ease.

As attention hones in upon the heart area, there is the experience
of coming home. The long search for peace and happiness comes to
an end. The theme of homecoming threads its way through most
spiritual traditions. In the New Testament, for example, Jesus tells
the parable of the prodigal son. The younger of two sons asks his
father for his share of the family's estate and leaves for a distant land,
only to squander his wealth in wild living. When he becomes desti-
tute, he comes to his senses and resolves to return home to his father
and to work as one of the servants. Then the author of the book of
Luke reports Jesus saying:

But while he [the son] was still a long way off, his father saw him and was filled with compassion for him; he ran to his son, threw his arms around him and kissed him. The son said to him, "Father I have sinned against heaven and against you. I am no longer worthy to be called your son." But the father said to his servants, "Quick! Bring the best robe and put it on him. Put a ring on his finger and sandals on his feet. Bring the fattened calf and kill it. Let's have a feast and celebrate. For this son of mine was dead and is alive again; he was lost and is found." So they began to celebrate.[2]

This profound parable describes the archetypal journey of attention from the head to the heart. Near the end of his futile search for happiness in the world, the prodigal son is deeply humbled and willing to serve. From a great distance, his father sees him returning and runs to embrace him. He recognizes that his son, once dead and now alive, is spiritually reborn. In the same way, the heart patiently awaits the return of the wandering mind and extends itself when there is a humble and open state of attention. Once the mind knows its limits, it can rest in the fullness of the heart. It can come home.

The Hara

As crucial as the illumined heart is to the spiritual journey, it is both possible and necessary that open awareness saturates the entire body. Nothing can be left out if we are interested in the full embodiment of our true nature. Once the heart area has been liberated, attention continues to move downward into the area of the belly, or the *hara*. The term *hara* is mostly used in Japanese martial arts such as aikido and meditative traditions such as Zen. It refers to a vital energy center that resides below the navel in the lower belly. While the hara appears to be distinct from the subtle energy centers known as *chakras*, which I will say more about later in this chapter, it appears to encompass the three lowest chakras, from the base of the spine through the solar plexus area. As the hara awakens, we experience a growing sense of profound inner stability. We feel our genuine autonomy, our capacity to stand fully on our own feet even as we know our deep interconnection with life.

The hara is sometimes called the existential center because it is intimately involved with themes of existence and survival. It is usually the location of the final stronghold of resistance to surrendering to a deeply awakened life. The separate sense of self is deeply rooted in the body and deeply identified with the body. We think we are just this body. Yet our physical body is only a small part of who we are. Or we could say that our "body" is much greater than we can imagine, that it encompasses all of life.

We imagine that we are in control of our lives, when the range of our control is extremely limited. We think that we are the doer of our actions, even though much of our action is unconsciously mediated or heavily influenced by our genes or upbringing. Consider your health, family heritage, cultural conditioning, and attachment style. We all have a very normal and deeply conditioned tendency, as Antonio Damasio noted, to think that we own our body, are located inside of it, and that we are the free agent of our actions (see chapter 1). These are primal elements of our sense of identity. However, when we carefully investigate, we discover that we are unable to verify any of these common-sense assumptions. This dawning awareness, especially if it is more than a mental recognition, is deeply disorienting for most of us. Sometimes it is terrifying.

Does our survival depend upon being in control? It doesn't seem to. Most of the control that we think we have or need is illusory. We are like children on the Disneyland ride Autopia, who turn the wheel imagining we are steering our bright little car when all along it is being guided by a rail hidden beneath us. There is a current of life that is carrying us, and we can sense and feel it if we can slow down enough. Rather than willfully muscling or anxiously thrashing our way through life, we can learn to attune with this current and ride it, much like a surfer catching a wave. This requires a deep, quiet grounding in and through the body that includes a sense of the hara.

Sensing the Hara

Set aside ten minutes and find a quiet, comfortable place
to sit. Close your eyes and take a few slow, deep breaths.
Place your hand over your lower abdomen and familiarize
yourself with the sensation of touch here. Imagine that you
can directly breathe in and out from this area. Mainly focus
on sensation. If your attention hops onto a train of thought,
gently bring it back to the lower belly and the sensation of
touch and breath.

After ending the short session of sitting, walk around
slowly for a few minutes and notice how your posture and
movements may be subtly affected. ●

The Energy Body and the Chakras

As our capacity to sense into the interior of the body grows and refines,
our experience of the body changes. The body no longer feels so numb,
solid, dense, and static. It begins to feel more alive, fluid, and spacious.
It starts to *feel* more like energy. Many contemplative traditions call
this the *energy body*. While it may sound esoteric, I'm pretty sure that
you have experienced it yourself.

One of the most common forms of experiencing the energy body
is also one of the most painful: heartbreak. If you have ever deeply
loved someone and then lost them through a breakup or death, you
know the range of feeling in the heart, from a hollow ache to a
wrenching, stabbing contraction. Remember Candice's image of the
sword in the heart? You may have also experienced its opposite, when
you have fallen in love and felt a great opening. In either case, you
feel the sensation in the center of the chest. What exactly is this? It
is not the physical heart, lungs, or musculature, although all of these
may be indirectly affected. Clearly, there is some center of feeling
that localizes in the center of the chest. The classic theme of the heart
breaking or opening, endlessly described in popular songs, movies,
and stories, is a very accessible example of how we experience the
energy body.

The energy body is a bridge between our ordinary, solid, and apparently separate humanness and infinite awareness—between the particular and the universal. To use more theological language, it is the way we *sense* the presence of the divine in our ordinary lives. Tibetan Buddhists call it the *Sambhogakaya*. As humans, we are multidimensional, and the energy body is an important intermediary realm of experience that lies between the poles of form and formlessness. As we attune with the energy body, we feel more intimately connected with others and with the depths of life.

Eckhart Tolle, author of *The Power of Now*, writes beautifully about how attuning with the energy body opens us to true listening:

> When listening to another person, don't just listen
> with your mind, listen with your whole body. Feel
> the energy field of your inner body as you listen. That
> takes attention away from thinking and creates a still
> space that enables you to truly listen without the mind
> interfering. You're giving the other person space—space
> to be. It is the most precious gift that you can give. . . .
> Being in touch with your inner body creates a clear space
> of no-mind within which the relationship can flower.[3]

After decades of sitting with people, I find Tolle's description very resonant. When I listen, it feels like listening is happening with the whole body. There is a feeling of openness, availability, and great intimacy—in a word, love.

The energy body is a spectrum of inner, whole-body sensitivity. Within it are certain centers and a central channel. In my opinion, Indian yogic and Tibetan Buddhist traditions have mapped these the most accurately, although we find alternative maps and accounts in most of the world's mystical traditions. For me, the energy body continues to be an unfolding discovery. As I share its inner cartography with you, it is important for you to know that it is not essential to experience these subtle energies directly. It is enough if you know their most important qualities—love and wisdom.

The Central Channel and the Chakras

There is a central channel of subtle energy—a life current—that runs through the core of the body. It is known as *kundalini* or serpent energy in yogic traditions because it has been likened to a coiled snake at the base of the spine that gradually unfolds upward. Imagine a cobra rising up out of a basket, and you get the image. There are certain practices that are used to awaken this energy, but I wouldn't recommend them. Trying to manipulate this primal energy with the goal-oriented mind carries significant risks. Life takes care of itself quite wisely, and it is enough to simply sense and attune with whatever energetic shifts are spontaneously happening.

As the central channel of the energy body awakens and is illumined, we feel a deep current of aliveness and intimacy. It is not the aliveness of external excitement and stimulation, the drama that we are so often and easily addicted to. Rather, it is a deeply quiet vibrancy that we sense in the core of our being. We also sense an uprightness or verticality, a lively feeling of the eternal now that coexists with the flux of time. This upright, vertical sensation is directly related to the marker of inner alignment that I mentioned in the introduction and will explore in depth in chapter 6. There is a felt sense of intimacy with all of the forms of life, not only the exotically beautiful ones such as the birds of paradise of New Guinea with their fanciful, luminous tail feathers, but also with all of the familiar people and ordinary things around us. This intimacy extends to a sense of deep kinship with all beings. As the core of the body is illumined, so, too, quite surprisingly, is our sense of the world.

There are seven major energy centers or *chakras* (Sanskrit: wheels or discs) that are aligned along the central channel. They are traditionally numbered one through seven from the bottom up. Each is associated with a particular psycho-spiritual theme. We can sense them as distinct focal points of energy in the interior of our body. They are in varying states of openness or constriction depending upon circumstances and conditioning. I sometimes imagine them as sea anemones—delicate, multicolored undersea creatures that are in constant flux with the tidal surge of experience. As they open or close, we are more or less in touch with their essential qualities. Consider the vastly different experience of life when your heart feels open or closed. If we attend to the chakras with patience, affectionate attention, and curiosity, they gradually flower. We become like gardeners to our inner sensitivity.

First Chakra: Safety

The first, or root, chakra is located at the base of the spine and is concerned with issues of physical and psychological survival. When it is open and clear, we feel a sense of stability and groundedness. We may also sometimes sense an upwelling current of life energy arising from the ground. Our felt sense of the ground has multiple levels and stages, which I will discuss in detail in chapter 5. We can feel grounded physically, emotionally, energetically, and spiritually. As we more deeply explore the first chakra, a sense of these subtle dimensions of groundedness opens and deepens.

This energy center contracts whenever our core sense of self or our body feels threatened. Early trauma originating from serious illness or accidents, the death or long absence of a primary caretaker, and/or physical and emotional abuse and neglect can all leave a strong impact on this center. Insecure, avoidant, or disorganized attachment styles of parenting (see chapter 1) also compromise the first chakra. They can contribute to an underlying feeling of terror and a subtle energetic contraction at the base of the spine.

This profound fear can take various forms, depending upon its origin, yet the imagined end is always the same: death—by fatal abandonment ("I will be all alone"), attack ("I will be grievously injured"), engulfment ("I will be swallowed or suffocated and will lose myself"), or fragmentation ("I will fall apart and go crazy"). The physical sensation is a subtle shakiness and instability at the base of the spine, as if the rug could be pulled out at any moment. This shakiness may be initially masked by numbness, which makes it hard to sense into the lower half of the body and to feel any connection to the earth at all.

This terror tends to be strongly repressed. We will usually need to feel some degree of safety and support before we are willing to reencounter the deepest layers of it. However, it can sometimes be flushed out into the open after a sudden spiritual awakening, which can be a very tumultuous and overwhelming experience. Long meditation retreats can also occasionally trigger the uncovering of this deeply unsettling psychological material. For this reason, retreat leaders would do well to understand this phenomenon and have resources available to deal with it.

The terror of psychological annihilation and the terror of physical annihilation are closely linked. Although the two are distinct, they tend to overlap since our sense of self is so strongly identified with our physical body. As we start to awaken from the trance of the separate self, it can feel like we are losing all of our familiar ground and all of our points of reference. It can feel like we are dying. In a certain sense, we are. We are dying to who we think we are. We are dying as an apparent separate self, as an object among other objects, as an idea.

The conditioned mind can confuse this dissolution of the self with actual physical death. It will project old stories and their accompanying feelings onto this unknown openness. The dark, vibrant silence of no self may take on the guise of an abandoning or engulfing parent. One of my clients with a history of abandonment encountered this vast space and envisioned herself as an astronaut whose lifeline had been cut from the mother ship as she spun away into a dark, cold void. Another client with a history of engulfment experienced the same dark space to be fiercely invasive and devouring. Sometimes we can see through these veils of projection quickly; other times we will strongly recoil and then slowly work through them. A lot depends upon the readiness and interest of the explorer. It takes courage to go forward when we have this kind of psychological background.

There is a reason that most of us do not easily discover our true nature. The conditioning against this can be quite strong. Above all, as an apparently separate self, we want to be safe. In the end, though, we discover that our deepest safety comes from trusting our open awareness. Everything else that we rely upon falls away. Even the earth shudders and cracks open at times. I suspect that, aside from the obvious terror that earthquakes induce on a physical level, they are also deeply disquieting to the psyche for another reason: if we can't trust the solidity of the very earth upon which we stand, what can we trust? What is our deepest ground?

EXPERIMENT *Exploring the Chakras*

Set aside ten minutes, find a quiet place, and then bring your attention to the base of your spine. Imagine that you're breathing directly into and out of this energy center. Take a few minutes to allow your attention to settle here.

Without trying to change anything, notice how open or closed this center feels. Are there any emotions associated with this area? Do any images or memories spontaneously arise? Are you aware of any beliefs that go with this area?

Bring your attention out of this individual center and into the whole body before you end.

I invite you to do the same exploration for each of the other chakras. ◉

Second Chakra: Sensuality

The second chakra is located in the lower abdomen, between the navel and the genitals. We usually sense it most clearly as a radiant warmth during sexual arousal. It has a nurturing, generative, deeply sensual, life-giving quality that includes but goes far beyond sex. It also manifests as physical playfulness, spontaneous movement, and the love of physical touch. I can feel it when I pet my adorable, long-haired, black and white cat as he lies purring on my chest, take a beautiful hike through the forests and wildflowers at Point Reyes National Seashore along the California coast, or go for a refreshing swim and float in a lake—physical delight!

The second chakra will contract when we have been sexually abused or, to a lesser degree, when we have been exposed to inappropriate sexual attention and energy as a child, even when nothing has happened physically. In either case, a sexual boundary has been crossed on some level, and we react by shutting down and freezing in this area. Since these boundary violations also feel very unsafe, the first chakra is often affected, too. Contraction of the second chakra can also result from shaming and repressing sexual feelings. Sometimes the center can become overly active when we feel that sex is the only way that we can get affection and attention from others. Some people have naturally stronger sensual centers than others and may find that their sexuality and sensuality are an important expression of and portal to their essential nature.

Third Chakra: Interpersonal Power

The third chakra is located at the solar plexus, just below the diaphragm. It is often referred to as the power chakra, yet all of the energy centers are concerned with the radiance of some kind of particular power. I have found that the third chakra directly relates to *interpersonal* power—how we influence and are influenced by others in relationship. The personal will seems to be largely centered here. Our ability to set appropriate interpersonal boundaries—saying what we want and don't want, need and don't need—localizes here. Often anger and rage are stored here when we have been unable to set healthy boundaries.

The more empowered we feel, the less rage we experience. This is as true for groups as it is for individuals. To stay in balance and navigate our daily life, we need our *no* as much as our *yes,* much as we need both red and green lights to safely drive. In this sense, our *no* is as life-affirming as our *yes.* We won't feel safe opening to life unless we are confident that we can set clear boundaries. For this reason, the first and third chakras often work closely together. As we feel more fundamentally secure in our self and in life, we are able to express ourselves more directly and to set appropriate boundaries. Doing so reinforces our sense of safety.

Some spiritual seekers are very confused around the issue of boundaries, because they imagine that spiritual realization and living at one with life means that they should or will live without any boundaries. While boundaries are irrelevant on the level of formless essence, on the level of form, clear boundaries are essential for healthy functioning. It is important not to confuse levels. Awakening does not mean merging.

Interestingly, it becomes much easier to set flexible and adaptive individual boundaries as we discover who we really are. As we intuit an underlying unity with life, we also further differentiate on an individual level. The less that we protect or project a self-image, the more free we feel to be as we are—unique, yet not special in terms of feeling better than anyone else. As we get out of the business of manipulating others or ourselves, we learn to navigate our needs and desires in relationships much more directly and simply. We tend to be generous and are able to set limits. Likewise, we stop pressuring others to change. We mature out of being either doormats or bullies.

The third chakra, along with the fourth, is a major emotional center. When emotions have been either over- or underregulated, this center contracts. For example, if anger was never directly expressed in our family of origin or if we were subjected to uncontrollable rage, the effect will be similar—a shutting down in the solar plexus due to repression or fear. While anger sometimes has a legitimate role to play in our lives, it is often overused as a defense against more vulnerable feelings of hurt, fear, or shame. Shame also localizes here in the upper abdomen, as well as in the heart area, paralyzing our willingness to take risks in order to learn and grow. Shame and fear are often tightly interwoven; we are ashamed of our fear and afraid of our shame. The fear of public humiliation is a very common example of this connection.

Fourth Chakra: Love

The fourth chakra, or heart center, is located in the center of the chest, distinct from the physical heart on the left. This highly sensitive center governs a wide range of issues including love and acceptance, self-esteem, compassion, kindness, joy, grief, gratitude, and a sense of the whole of life. When our hearts are closed, we feel isolated, disconnected, and despairing, with a deep sense of alienation from our self and others. When our hearts are open, we feel the opposite—grateful, hopeful, and deeply connected with the whole of life. We are able to give and receive love freely.

I find that the heart center has three distinct levels: ego, soul, and self (sometimes capitalized as *Self* to distinguish it from the ego). As attention deepens into the heart area and approaches the back of the heart, subtler levels of this chakra come into our awareness. Generally speaking, the impact of earlier experiences is found at deeper levels. An exploration of these levels is like an archaeological dig. The deeper you go, the earlier the material you will find.

The ego level runs quite deep and is concerned with how we think and feel about ourselves. It is where we hold the core feelings about ourselves, along with the beliefs related to those feelings. Am I good enough? Am I acceptable just as I am? Am I lovable or even likable? Am I worthy of respect? Or am I lacking or flawed in some fundamental way? These imprints often are formed early in our lives and are based on our upbringing. Attachment styles and trauma can have a big impact. Sometimes our hearts will close incrementally when we face ongoing neglect and misunderstanding as children. We gradually give up trying to connect and retreat into our own world. Other times the heart slams shut like an iron gate when there has been a major breach of trust or an enormous loss. In either case, we unknowingly make ourselves a prisoner of our own defense, trapped in a prison of our own making. We bury the precious treasure of our sensitivity to protect it from others, and then we forget about it. To protect ourselves, it seems that we must lose touch with our sensitivity, at least for a while.

Reclaiming this buried treasure requires that we feel at least some of the pain that caused us to close our heart in the first place. It is much like the thawing of frozen ground or the reawakening of a numbed limb—there are often some pins and needles before there is warmth or feeling. This thawing of the heart can happen when we meet good friends or find a loving partner. An attuned psychotherapist can also help facilitate this melting. Because the wounding of this level of the heart came from deficient relationships, the healing will come through reparative ones.

The soul level lies at the very back of the heart and is sometimes experienced as a subtle, intense point of light. It corresponds to the sharing of our unique gifts. When we do express this level of ourselves, we feel like a well-played instrument. Often this sharing, this deep expression of our unique way of being, takes the form of an archetype, such as a healer, teacher, nurturer, leader, artist, mother, father, or warrior, or some combination of these. While this soulful expression rarely makes the national headlines, it feels deeply creative, internally congruent with our deepest nature, and inherently meaningful to us. We feel that we are doing our life's work, as Corinne sensed at the beginning of this chapter.

The back of the heart opens up into the unbounded self. Here we know ourselves as pure, universal being. We are awake, aware presence, free of all attributes; we are not someone in particular, we simply are. This level of being goes beyond our individuality, either egoic or soulful. It can be spoken of poetically as the great or cosmic heart—that which is capable of holding the collective suffering of humanity. This nonlocalized great heart is profoundly silent, timeless, and deeply compassionate. Our argument with reality ends here. Everything is accepted just as it is. When our attention rests here, we have the deep sense that all is well, no matter what.

Fifth Chakra: Honest Self-Expression

The fifth chakra is located in the middle of the throat and is concerned with self-expression. How well do we literally give voice to our truth? How well do we sing our song? Expressing our truth is not a matter of volume, but rather of clarity and congruence with our inner knowing. A calm, quiet voice that stays close to the facts and speaks from the authority of a deeper truth ultimately has much greater power than one that is loud, reactive, and confused. Gandhi is someone who exemplified this truth. When this center opens, we are able to speak truth to power.

Telling the truth as we know it—the unarguable truth of our own experience that is free of judgment and blame—is a high art.

It requires vulnerability, self-responsibility, and integrity. It also requires us to be equally willing to invite and to allow others to do the same. This is the beginning of an honest dialogue. We don't really know where this invitation to honesty will lead. A truly honest exchange can feel very risky to our image-maintenance project and to those relationships that are built upon false appearances. We can feel out of control when we really start telling the truth. Doing so is a rigorous spiritual practice. Try being scrupulously honest for a day and notice how you do.

When I work with couples, this is my main focus. What is the truth of their relationship? Once people stop blaming each other and defending themselves, dropping their spears and shields, an honest assessment of the relationship can begin. How well can they meet and understand one another as they are? What is the most natural form of the relationship? Are they better suited as lovers or as friends?

Deception has deep evolutionary roots because it can enhance immediate physical survival. Nearly every species in nature has astonishingly creative ways to disguise itself in order to eat and not be eaten. Opossums play dead, butterfly wings are ornamented to look like large predatory eyes, chameleons change colors to blend in with their environment, lions hunt from the shadows, and chimps try to hide their food stashes from their group's alpha male. Humans are no exception. Aside from telling outright lies, we are often shading the truth with omissions and exaggerations that put us in a better light. We are afraid that the truth will get us in trouble. There is a strong tension in us between wanting to stay safe and wanting to be honest and open, between deception (of ourselves and others) and integrity. Every time we choose truth-telling over deception, we connect more deeply with our true nature. Our *true* nature is truthful.

Truth-telling includes the freedom to feel our emotions and to express them when it is appropriate. Often sadness or anger can feel chronically choked off, as if there are actual hands around our throat throttling us. This can happen when feelings have been either strongly repressed or explosively expressed in our family of origin. A wave of feeling will rise up and then fall back when there is a strong blockage in the throat chakra. Sometimes constriction in this area can come from having been threatened with severe punishment or even death if we were to reveal a dark family secret, such as sexual abuse. More commonly, we hold back our self-expression because we imagine that we are not interesting, valuable, or good enough. We may have concluded early on that it is better to mute ourselves than to risk humiliation and rejection. It takes courage to find our true voice and then share it. Doing so is an essential part of the creative process.

Sixth Chakra: Clarity

The sixth chakra is located between and slightly above the eyebrows and is sometimes called the third eye. It is associated with clarity, discernment, insight, and understanding. This center is most obviously active when we recognize and see beyond our limiting beliefs.

All of us construct, usually unconsciously, a view of ourselves and the world. It is a story about who we are and what this world is. This subconscious story orients and guides how we feel and act. For instance, based upon your experience of growing up in your family, you might believe that you are not good enough and that the world is an uncaring, unwelcoming place. You might believe that you are powerless and that the world is very threatening and dangerous. Alternatively, you may have an inflated view that you are especially gifted and valuable and that you deserve special treatment and recognition from others. These stories are often deeply ingrained and quite powerful, especially when they are operating outside our conscious awareness. When we are triggered, they can erupt from the depths of the psyche like a breaching whale. They may also more quietly influence our choice of a partner and a career; for example, we believe that we should settle for less because no one will really love or value us as we are. Additionally, and perhaps more importantly, these limiting beliefs become an integral part of our core identity.

I think it is impossible to live an ordinary life without some kind of view of our self and the world. Yet it *is* possible to recognize and stand back from our view and see it as though it is a pair of glasses that we can put on and take off. When we are keenly discerning, we can see the lens through which we view life. However, when we are unable to do this and we *identify* with our view of ourselves and the world, we live in a kind of trance that creates suffering for ourselves and others. When this happens, we are like a disturbed sleepwalker who is lost in a bad dream.

My clients will occasionally wonder if they will go insane if they let go of their core limiting beliefs. Who will they be, and how will they function if they no longer see themselves as flawed, deficient some-bodies? I reassure them that the opposite is happening—that they are going sane.

There is a subtle tension in the brain when we are identified with our limiting thoughts. A more limited view creates the felt sense of greater energetic contraction in both the front and back of the head. It may feel like we are wearing one of those heavy medieval helmets with a tiny viewing slot. Conversely, the clearer and more reality-based our view becomes, the more we feel a subjective sense of spaciousness in and around the head. It can feel as if a helmet has been lifted off. My clients sometimes report feeling as if the back of their heads have opened up into a vast space, echoing William Blake's famous observation from *The Marriage of Heaven and Hell*: "If the doors of perception were cleansed everything would appear to man as it is, Infinite. For man has closed himself up, till he sees all things thro' narrow chinks of his cavern."

When we see beyond the "narrow chinks" of our limiting beliefs, perception *is* cleansed, and we *can* sense the infinite. Interestingly, our physical vision may also clarify and widen; objects may appear clearer, colors brighter. When we are convinced of a core limiting belief about ourselves—for example, that we are deeply flawed and unlovable—we imprison our sense of self and then desperately try to escape via distraction, numbing, or denial. At some point, we may realize that there is no escape; instead, we see that the apparent prison is not real. We awaken from our dream of mistaken identity and see that we have taken ourselves to be someone or something that we are not.

This awakening usually requires self-inquiry—a deep, heartfelt process of discernment. We begin to wonder: Who am I really? Is this belief about myself or the world really true? What do I know for certain? Undoing or deconstructing our cherished view can be both liberating and disorienting. In time, though, we will find ourselves at ease with not knowing who we are or what this world is. While our mind may initially fear being unable to know, it will eventually be grateful to relax. We can safely drop the old set of clothes, the old misidentities, and be naked.

The truth is that we don't really know who we are, and we don't need to. We discover that we can live in the world quite happily and effectively on a genuine need-to-know basis. Being willing to not know opens up new ways of seeing, feeling, and responding. It is more honest, creative, and a lot more enjoyable! Not knowing allows for the recovery of our native innocence and the spontaneous emergence of a different kind of knowing.

Seventh Chakra: Waking Up

The seventh chakra is located at the very top of the head and is sometimes called the crown chakra. It is associated with awakening, inner freedom, and soulful guidance. It serves as a portal to waking up out of identification with any thought, feeling, or sensation so that we know unbounded freedom. When this center opens, we know ourselves as pure, open awareness—free from any definition.

When I was on a small retreat with Adyashanti in 2001 and recognized infinity looking out simultaneously from both of our eyes, it felt like an inner skylight shattered. There was no longer a sense of being a localized observer. I knew myself as the light of awareness free of all form, no longer bounded by space and time. It is a clear sense of timeless presence that does not belong to anyone. "I" was experiencing this freedom, but there was no longer a locatable I. It was as if the top of the bottle had popped off, and the genie who had thought he was contained inside discovered that he was actually the open space within which the bottle appears. It is a transcendent realization: "I am not in this body; this body is in me as spacious awareness."

The hallmark quality of this opening is inner freedom. Yet it is a negative freedom—a *freedom from* form. It is not yet a *freedom to* enter into form. A subtle duality continues between an unbounded knower and the apparently bounded known. While one's self may feel infinite, the "world" appears to be finite and subtly separate. This distinction may be overlooked during the first blush of awakening. To know one's self as infinite is a precious and liberating revelation. It is, so to speak, no small thing. But it also is not everything. The whole world is waiting to be revealed.

An initial *waking up* is followed by a *waking down,* so that the entire body is saturated with and liberated by this expansive awareness.[4] A downward movement of open awareness follows, which requires us to bring our ordinary human life into accord with our true nature. Sometimes it can be a difficult and lengthy process, depending upon the kind and degree of prior conditioning and the amount of inner work that we have already done. In any case, this process of waking down and coming into accord with our true nature requires a great deal of vulnerability and honesty.

One of the most common ways that I sense the seventh, or crown, chakra functioning during my work with clients is when they experience a downpouring of intuitive guidance, as if it is coming from a higher realm. I experienced this recently when one of my clients, a spiritually oriented young man who had struggled socially and academically through his first two years of college, began to clearly express the sense of what he wanted and needed to focus on in his third year: keeping up with his class assignments, broadening and deepening his friendships, regularly exercising, and attending to the sense of presence. It was as if he was getting his subtle marching orders for all levels—intellectual, emotional, physical, and spiritual. I'd never heard or felt him to be so clear and focused. An inner direction—both practical and soulful—was unfolding, and it felt as though it was being delivered by a descending current from above. Could this be why so many people look upward when they are seeking divine guidance?

Summary

While you may or may not have sensed the specific energy centers that I have just described, you're probably familiar with most of the issues that they govern. For example, you may have experienced terror at some point in your life and felt a sense of shakiness in your legs and a lack of groundedness. Conversely, you may have at one time felt a deep sense of stability, groundedness, and connection with the earth. These are both related to the first, or root, chakra. Perhaps you have had moments of great sensual or sexual expansiveness or, alternatively, felt very numb or shut down this way—the second chakra's domain. You have almost certainly wrestled with how to set appropriate boundaries with others and how to honor your core needs and feelings while respecting those of others. These are third chakra issues. You have probably experienced times of self-acceptance and self-hatred, joy and grief, or loved someone deeply and lost them. These are issues of the fourth or heart chakra. You have succeeded or failed to tell the truth many times, expressed or repressed your deep feelings—all fifth chakra themes. You have been insightful or insightless, brilliantly clear or deeply confused, lost in your thoughts or able to witness them like clouds passing in the sky—the domain of the sixth chakra. And you may have glimpsed a transcendent freedom and realized that you are beyond any definition—a seventh chakra function.

The felt sense is the whole-body sense of something that is not yet clear to the conscious mind. The capacity for felt sensing is inherent in you. The more that you slow down, breathe, clear the mind, and begin to sense into the core of your body, the more available the felt sense will be to your conscious awareness. Your devotion to this kind of listening will tune the instrument of your deep sensitivity. Unless you are a natural at felt sensing, it usually takes some patience and heartfelt practice to develop it. In time, your attention will gradually be able to drop down and into your body whenever you want to access your sense of inner knowing. You will get quiet and tune in without thinking about it.

As your ability for felt sensing expands, a wide range of subtle perception flowers. This may or may not include sensing your energy centers and energy flows. Your perceptions may take the form of images, songs, or just a direct knowing. The form is not important. What is important is to be in touch with your inner knowing, to have a sense of what is in or out of accord with yourself.

PART II

reducing the noise

It is hard to sense the signal of inner knowing when our attention is absorbed in a reactive feeling, somatic contraction, and limiting belief. I think of this as "noise" in the system. Rather than trying to rid ourselves of our reactions—which is a reaction itself—there is a way to be with them so that they become portals to our deeper knowing. Our distress can be taken as a wake-up call to pay careful and affectionate attention to whatever needs it. If the distress is too great, we will need to resource ourselves first in order to skillfully be with it. This resourcing may include remembering positive experiences and calling in inner or outer guides and protectors. Our true nature as open awareness is our greatest resource.

Most of our emotional reactions and somatic contractions originate in our unclear thinking, particularly our core limiting beliefs. It is important to recognize these beliefs and to inquire into their truth from a place of deep heartfelt knowing. It is also helpful to be able to dialogue with the inner critic and to witness thoughts.

3

being with experience:
shadows as portals

*One does not become enlightened
by imagining figures of light, but by
making the darkness conscious.*

CARL JUNG

Rose had attended a retreat that I co-led a few years before and felt ready to come in for a series of individual sessions. During our first meeting, she reported feeling burdened by a deep sadness, which she had carried her whole life, despite having a good marriage, close relationships with her adult children, and a satisfying career as an artist. She was afraid that the depth of her sadness would swallow her if she opened up to it. She said that it felt like an extremely dense weight in the center of her chest.

After she shared a bit of her family-of-origin history, which centered around having a highly preoccupied mother who was emotionally distant and unavailable, I had a sense of where we needed to go. Knowing that Rose trusted me and feeling the immediate rapport that we had established, I asked her if she would be willing to let herself feel and sense this deep sadness and intense contraction in her heart area as she simultaneously maintained a soft gaze with me. She immediately agreed, and we dove into the sadness together.

I encouraged her to feel her sadness and to sense the sharp contraction in her chest fully as she maintained the current of contact with me. There was an immediate deepening of attention, the pain sharpened, and she began to cry. She felt an intense wave of shame pass through her about being so emotionally vulnerable and needy. She felt like an unloved and unlovable little girl who was completely exposed. She also felt deeply seen and held with kindness and understanding by me.

After a few minutes, the contraction softened and her tears stopped. Rose reported sensing a growing lightness in her heart area—a lightness that I also felt. Her eyes gradually cleared, and she smiled beautifully. She knew that her story of being unlovable was untrue. She also experienced a luminous sense of being. I felt as if I was witnessing an inner sunrise.

Rose's most shadowed area within her body, the center of her chest where the painful contraction was, turned out to be a direct portal to a sense of radiant being. What she most feared embracing became the entry point to an essential sense of self.

How can the most emotionally painful parts of our inner experience yield such light? Could there be an essential radiance within our darkest places? In this chapter I will explore how to be with our conditioned experiences, particularly difficult feelings and sensations, in a way that liberates them. Apparent obstacles become, as Rose discovered, doors to awakening.

Shadows as Portals

Small children are vulnerable and feel everything deeply. They also lack discernment and mature empathy. They don't understand the impact that their own egocentric impulses, desires, and actions have upon others or why people, particularly their parents, act as they do. For instance, if children are treated badly, they assume that they are bad. If they are not loved or attended to, they assume that they are not worth being cared for. If they are constantly told how special they are because of their parent's narcissistic need to have a perfect child, they believe this distorted reflection.

A child's view of the world is naïve. Primary caretakers are like gods—huge, powerful, and unpredictable beings. This perception is amplified if children have a fundamentalist religious upbringing and learn to see God as an all-knowing and vengeful male. When my first wife, Linda, was approaching the end of her life due to pulmonary hypertension from a congenital heart defect, she reencountered this archaic worldview. Despite being a longtime meditator and student of Indian and Tibetan wisdom teachings, she was plagued by fears of going to hell because of something she had reasoned out when she attended summer Bible school as an eight-year-old. At the time, she was staying with her kind and devout grandmother. One day at Bible school, she learned the following passage from the Gospel of Matthew:

> When the Son of Man comes in his glory, and all the
> angels with him, he will sit on his glorious throne.
> All the nations will be gathered before him, and he
> will separate the people one from another as a shepherd
> separates the sheep from the goats. He will put the
> sheep on his right and the goats on his left. . . . Then
> he will say to those on his left, "Depart from me, you
> who are cursed, into the eternal fire prepared for the
> devil and his angels."[1]

As a result, Linda decided that her grandmother—certainly the holier of the two of them—was one of the sheep who would go to heaven, and she was a goat who would go to hell. This terrifying belief, long buried in the subconscious, persisted until the day before she died. When it lifted, Linda became like a joyful little girl.

EXPERIMENT *Discovering Your Parents' Vulnerability*

Take a moment to consider how you experienced your parent or parents when you were young. When did you begin to realize that they were vulnerable human beings struggling with their own shortcomings? ●

As children, we assume that whatever we are experiencing, no matter how extreme, is normal. Further, in the early years, we unconsciously absorb all kinds of impulses that are in the psychological field around us. Some of these impulses are nurturing and helpful; others are toxic. As a result, unless we are raised by unusually well-attuned parents, we tend to shut down our natural sensitivity, as Rose did when she closed her heart after many painful attempts to reach out and connect with her mother. It is simply too painful to stay open and tolerate poor attunement, trauma, neglect, or abuse. We reflexively learn to protect ourselves. The ensuing fortress that we build subtly imprisons us as an adult.

Defenses take a myriad of forms, some of which are hard to recognize. It is useful to see which ones we adopted early on and still use. For example, in order to get a grip on ourselves, we may deaden or freeze areas of painful emotional sensitivity. As a little boy, I learned to unconsciously tighten my diaphragm and constrain my breath in order not to feel shame or fear. When you think about it, freezing is actually a very efficient way to preserve life; consider the foods in your freezer. Much of my conventional psychotherapy work involves helping people to thaw out from frozen patterns of thought, feeling, and sensation.

We may dissociate, living in a space somewhere outside of our body, so that we don't feel what is happening within and around us. I am currently working with a traumatized client who reports that a part of him split off when he was eight years old and still lives in a cave as an outcast isolated from the world. This vital part, wounded and frozen, like a soldier left for years in a foxhole on a winter battlefield, is gradually making its way back into his body as it feels safe to do so. Another of my clients, in the face of repeated physical and sexual abuse as a girl, found refuge beneath a huge imaginary boulder. During our inner excavation work, we discovered what at first appeared to be the flattened and lifeless body of a little girl. In fact, the child was in a kind of deep sleep. In time, she reawakened and came out of hiding.

While some people are interested in having an out-of-body experience, many have never had a fully in-the-body experience, where they feel deeply at ease in their bodies and sense the body's natural fluid, alive, and open way of being. If you can't remember most of your childhood, it is almost certain that you were, for good reason, spending a lot of time out of the body in a dissociated state. It was simply too emotionally painful to be there.

There are many other types of defenses. We may avoid contact and conflict, withdrawing inwardly so that we will not be attacked or abandoned. We may be quick to leave others before we are left, exiting a relationship at the first signs of danger. We may adopt a placating strategy toward others in order to feel safe, and then we feel inwardly resentful for being used. Alternatively, we may take an aggressive stance and use anger and rage as a way to keep others at a distance. In more extreme cases, we may split ourselves and others into good and bad and be unable to tolerate either closeness or distance, aching for contact but unable to trust it when it is offered.

With age we add layers to these earlier defenses as we medicate and distract ourselves with drugs, alcohol, food, sex, or too much work. Anything, including the spiritual search, can be used as a defense to avoid emotional pain and to try to feel better. Along the way, regardless of our conditioning, we become lost in the judging mind and gradually forget who we are, both emotionally and spiritually.

Defenses operate simultaneously on different levels of thought, feeling, and sensation. Somatically, our breathing constricts and our muscles tighten. Our highly sensitive energy body (see chapter 2) contracts like a turtle pulling into its shell. Emotionally, we lose touch with our more tender feelings and become lost in reactive ones. Mentally, our thinking becomes distorted or rigidly judgmental, prone to fantasy, denial, projection, or fanatic beliefs.

All of these defenses separate us from our true nature. We feel both a deep loss and a profound grief. The grief may puzzle us at first because we are unable to identify what has been lost. In time we realize that we are grieving the loss of our deepest self. In my client and mentoring work, I often encounter this existential grief, within which lies a deep yearning to come home to our native wholeness.

These defenses limit or even cripple our functioning as adults, undermining our attempts to find a suitable partner or rewarding work.

They block our creative flow and capacity for intimacy. Yet they served a vital purpose while we were growing up. At the time, they were the best ways that we knew to deal with an indifferent or hostile environment. They were intelligent attempts to adapt. For this reason, it is important that we not judge our defenses, but rather approach them with understanding and compassion. "Bless their little hearts," I will sometimes tell my clients.

The good news is that every defense is linked to an essential human quality. When we carefully follow a defense inward, we will discover what was being defended. We may first encounter shame, fear, or despair—everything that we originally didn't want to feel and tried to push away. However, sometimes with surprising speed, this underlying vulnerability becomes a portal to a greater resourcefulness, as Rose experienced. For example, if we follow the feeling of being unlovable inward, we will eventually discover that we are inherently lovable. If we explore doubt, we will discover a quiet confidence. Our fear will bring us to fearlessness. Shame will lead us to innocence. Over time, our shadowy defenses will reveal themselves to be allies that help point us to our essential qualities.

Our defenses are an interacting system of thoughts, feelings, and sensations. In most cases, our thinking, which is often subconscious, determines our feelings. For example, if on some level we believe that we are a worthless human being, we will feel worthless.

EXPERIMENT   *Observing the Impact of Negative Thoughts*

Take a few moments to entertain a negative thought about yourself and then think of its exact opposite. For example, "I am worthless" and then "I am worthwhile. I have value." Notice what you feel and sense with each opposing thought. How do they differ? ●

The self-critical thought will always generate a feeling of contraction on some level. We will also be able to sense a corresponding constriction in our body, usually in the heart center. We then take these feelings and sensations as evidence that we are worthless, thinking, "If I feel this way, it must be true." This is a common and critical error—we take the by-products of our thinking as proof of what is wrong with us. This is like unknowingly cutting our body with a knife and then interpreting the blood as evidence that we have a major unknown illness. We don't see that the bleeding originated from a self-inflicted wound.

As we think, so we feel. Our reactive feelings are usually the body's response to thought. They are by-products of a lack of clear seeing. Consider how strongly you may react emotionally and somatically during a nightmare and what a relief it is to wake up and realize that it was only a dream. Our distorted thinking creates a similar kind of nightmare during the waking state. We are often unaware of how our thinking mediates our experience. We have an experience and react without realizing that there has been an intermediary step of mental interpretation.

Think about how often you have misinterpreted someone else's intentions and upset yourself. "She is late because she doesn't care about me," you may think, and then feel hurt, angry, or depressed before learning that your friend was stuck in heavy traffic. If you don't get a response to a text message or a phone call, you may judge your friend as being inconsiderate or wonder if you have offended him, only to learn later that he never got the message or was busy. We tend to take these potential slights or disappointments personally.

How often have we been advised "not to take it personally"—a profound wisdom teaching disguised as ordinary advice? When self-inquiry goes very deep, we recognize that nothing that happens to us is actually personal. It is a surprising and very liberating discovery to see that we are not who we believe we are. The less attached we are to a story or image about ourselves, the more we are able to see things as they are. As we become clearer about who we are not—all of our stories and self-images—our thinking becomes increasingly clear, and our feelings become more stable and refined.

We are often unaware of how much our thinking affects our feelings because the interpretive lens of our self-view and worldview is largely hidden. In the next chapter, I will examine the power that our beliefs hold and how we can recognize and question them. For now, it is enough to note the highly influential role they play in creating and maintaining our defense systems.

As important as thoughts are, they are not always the primary source of our reactive feelings and sensations. Our nervous system and feelings are entrained with our mother's and primary caretaker's before we are born and throughout our childhood. When these natural bonds are impaired or broken early on through trauma or an attachment disorder (see chapter 1), our brain has not developed enough to formulate thoughts about the experience. There is simply the raw impact of the experience on our organism, largely unmediated by thought. In this case, thoughts will come later and be secondary to sensations and feelings. They may be used to codify and solidify our experience.

Being Intimate with Experience

How do you relate to your experience—particularly your more challenging or emotionally painful experiences? Do you welcome them, or do you try to distance yourself from them? Do you lean in, or do you lean away? Are you intimate with them or distant from them?

The path of distancing is well-worn and familiar: we judge ourselves or others, and then we attack, withdraw, or numb. These reactions are all variations of the classic defensive repertoire of fight, flight, or freeze. The path of welcoming our experience, of becoming intimate with it, is less familiar. While it seems riskier, it is far more rewarding.

We tend to instinctively avoid both physical and emotional pain. Who wants to feel worse? Yet when we realize that our pain is actually a message telling us to pay attention, we begin to approach our experience differently. I often tell my clients and students that their mental turmoil and emotional discomfort is a wake-up call—like an alarm clock sounding in the morning. Something within and around us wants and needs our careful attention.

Dis-ease is a signal to listen. I think this is true of suffering in general. Our deepest suffering comes from taking ourselves as a separate self. It seems that life is designed to accent this fact: the more self-centered we are, the greater we suffer. The more that we see through our egocentricity and let go, the less we suffer. It is like an elegant physics formula.

Life is inviting us to pay careful attention to our experience. The last decade has seen the rapid growth in the use of what is called mindfulness in psychotherapy and trainings for physical pain reduction. Once little known, mindfulness has entered into the mainstream through the pioneering work of Buddhist-influenced writers and researchers such as Jon Kabat-Zinn, Jack Kornfield, Richard Davidson, Rick Hanson, and Daniel Siegel, and psychologists such as Marcia Linehan, who founded Dialectic Behavior Therapy, and Steven Hayes, who created Acceptance and Commitment Therapy. Mindfulness generally refers to giving present-centered, nonjudgmental attention to an object of awareness, such as the breath or a painful sensation. It includes an attitude of openness and curiosity. While *mindfulness,* a once obscure term, has quickly become a coin of the realm, I prefer to call it *affectionate attention.* Whatever its name, this quality of attention is profoundly liberating.

This kind of warmly open, accepting, curious, and present-centered attention can be purposefully cultivated to an extent. As we saw in chapter 1, research shows that our brains can be trained to be attentive, with beneficial results. Neurons that fire together will wire together, as the saying goes. Neurological, mental, and emotional patterns from childhood can transform as a result of us being attentive to them and developing new ways of thinking and feeling. We can be grateful for the brain's neuroplasticity.

At the same time, it is important to recognize that our conditioned mind will never be able to unconditionally accept what is. The conscious mind always has a quiet background agenda to change or get rid of a troublesome experience by accepting it. One of my clients said to me, referring to a deep constriction in his body resulting from an early trauma, "Maybe I can love it away." This was conditional acceptance disguised as unconditional acceptance. I suggested that he just love his experience—period.

Whatever we resist persists—that is another inner law. We can sense when we are accepted and loved unconditionally by others. When this happens, we relax. And then, almost miraculously, we feel safe enough to open up like a flower bud in the warming sun. Our relationship to our inner experience is no different. Whatever we are resisting within ourselves senses the lack of full acceptance, no matter how subtle, and braces against it. We seem to be facing a great dilemma: if deep transformation only happens when there is unconditional acceptance and if the conditioned mind cannot accept unconditionally, what is there to do?

The good news is that there is an awareness in us that already accepts everything just as it is. This awareness is not of the mind, and it is not *mindful* in any ordinary sense of this word. It is certainly not about thinking, evaluating, or bargaining in any way. Instead, it tends to be centered in the heart area. It is heartful or no-mindful. Your deepest nature loves what is, just as it is.

How can we know this awareness firsthand? How do we recognize it? It is all about listening to and attuning with what is already here. We can start by relaxing.

EXPERIMENT *Being as You Are*

Find a comfortable place to sit where you will not be disturbed. Let yourself know that there is nothing that you need to do, think about, or solve for the next few minutes. You will have thoughts anyway, but it is nice to remind your mind that it is okay if your thinking is not productive.

You may want to prerecord the following instructions on your smartphone or other recording device and then listen to them. If you do, be sure to pace the instructions so there are long, silent pauses between the steps.

Close your eyes and take a few slow, deep breaths. Feel your feet on the ground. Feel the weight of your body in the chair and let yourself be held—by the chair, by gravity, by the earth. (Pause.)

Let your experience be as it is. There is nothing to change or achieve, no place inwardly or outwardly you need to go. It is enough simply to notice what you are experiencing. (Pause.)

Be aware of the sensations of your body, beginning with external sounds. Let your listening be completely receptive. Focus on the sensation of the sound rather than trying to name what it is. Let all sounds be as they are. (Pause.)

Be aware of the sensations of touch: first your hands and feet (pause), then your back, bottom, and legs. Let them be as they are. (Pause.)

Be aware of the interior of the trunk of your body, first your chest (pause) and then your belly (pause). Let them be as they are. (Pause.)

Feel the space inside your body (pause) and then around your body in all directions (pause). Let this sense of space be as it is. (Pause.)

Notice your emotions, if there are any. Notice how you sense them in your body (pause). Let them be as they are. (Pause.)

Notice your thoughts as you would observe clouds passing in the sky. Don't get involved with them; just notice them coming and going. (Pause.) Notice if they are in the form of words, images, or memories (pause), and if they are about the past or the future. (Pause.) Let your thoughts be as they are. (Pause.)

Notice that the one thing that has been consistent throughout your observation is the noticing itself. While the contents of awareness—your sensations, emotions, and thoughts—have been constantly changing, the context of awareness has not. Rest as this silent awareness. Let yourself be as you are. (Very long pause.) Rest here as long as you like.

When you are ready to bring your attention out, feel your hands and feet and then slowly open your eyes. Savor the sense of awareness for a minute before getting up. ●

This is a simple yet very potent disidentification experiment. We simply observe what we normally identify with, particularly our thoughts, and begin to familiarize ourselves experientially with a background awareness. This awareness is almost always overlooked; it quietly waits to be recognized as who we essentially are. It is simple, open, and empty of definition. There is nothing for the mind to grab onto here, so the conditioned mind tends to dismiss it. There is no way to know this awareness as we would know an object. Therefore, to the mind it is no-thing or nothingness—a blank state. Yet without it, there would be nothing; without this knowing awareness, there would be no perception at all. It does not take willful effort to recognize this awareness as our self. It does, however, require clear understanding and attunement—a kind of deep listening—in order for this recognition to be more than a superficial mental realization.

As we learn to deeply attune with and get the feel of this awareness, we may first discover that it has the qualities of openness, freedom, and pristine clarity. As our attunement with it continues to deepen, we will experience this awareness as having a warm, heartfelt quality. We will sense its loving and intimate nature and begin to realize that this awareness is intimate with everything. It knows everything as itself. This is the deepest dimension of love. This heartful awareness welcomes, accepts, and loves everything as an intimate expression of itself.

It seems that everything, in both our inner and outer worlds, wants to be consciously met by this awareness in order to be liberated. All of our apparent wounds and frozen places, individually and collectively, are waiting to be touched by the kindness and clarity that radiates from this awareness.

Spiritual or Mental Bypassing?

Spiritual bypassing, a term coined by existential psychologist John Welwood, refers to the tendency to avoid unresolved emotional issues, psychological wounds, and unfinished developmental tasks by pursuing spiritual practices and ideals, most notably the quest for enlightenment.[2] To me, it seems more accurate to call this tendency *mental bypassing* because it is the mind that uses the *idea* of spirituality to avoid being emotionally vulnerable. If we think of spirit as being solely transcendent, it is easy to fall into this trap. However, if we understand spirituality to mean that which is essential and not separate from anything, then spirit is not capable of bypassing anything—it is inherent in everything. It is the conditioned mind, not spirit, that resists reality.

Regardless of what we call it, bypassing or avoidance definitely happens, and it is frequently employed by spiritual seekers and teachers as a defense against being vulnerable. It shows up most visibly in the arena of personal relationships and around issues of intimacy. It is possible and common for attention to temporarily skip over troubled mental, emotional, and somatic layers and rest for a while in expansive states. As long as we don't try to closely interact with other people, we can remain peaceful. Meditation retreats, long solitary walks in the woods—no problem! But if we try to navigate an intimate relationship, all of the unfinished business of the heart floods to the surface.

It is easy to hide out in the big space of awareness and to avoid our more tender areas. We can keep ourselves at a safe distance from others, slightly or greatly removed from our human feelings and needs, with the idea that "I am no one" and certainly "I am none of these troublesome thoughts, feelings, or sensations." Spiritual teachings about detachment can fuel this avoidance.

It may be quite natural to first pursue and discover our true nature as pure awareness, empty of all definitions and content. Yet if we are interested in living this discovery in our ordinary lives, we will need to fully and intimately embrace the entirety of our experience, including our emotionally tender layers.

Resources for Being Intimate with Experience

How can we be more intimate with our experience? Over the years I have discovered a number of different ways that can help. Experiment and see what works for you.

Explore Being as You Are

As we become more familiar with the spacious, open awareness that is our home ground, we are much more available to be intimate with our experience as it is. This spacious and intimate awareness is our greatest resource. Without it, we are identified with our thoughts, feelings, and sensations and remain both fused with and confused by the contents of our awareness. When we know this awareness as our ground, as the essence of who we are—ungraspable as this may be to the mind—our inner experience begins to fall into place. We stop struggling with it, even as we remain keenly and intimately attentive. When the Zen master Bankei said, "All things are perfectly resolved in the Unborn," he was referring to this experience of open awareness.

Spend some time experimenting with the "Being as You Are" practice earlier in this chapter. Familiarize yourself experientially with this spacious, heartfelt, and intimate background awareness. Doing so will bring it more into the foreground of your daily life. The effects are generally subtle and will take time to unfold.

While a regular sitting meditation practice can be very beneficial, it is important that such a practice be approached in an innocent way, freshly, without a goal. It is a meditation of the heart, not the mind. It is enough for attention to rest in the heart area, not knowing.

Sense Space

A complementary practice to "Being as You Are" is to evoke a sense of space. My teacher Jean Klein, who was trained as a medical doctor, advised his students to attune with a sense of space before exploring an area of painful physical or emotional contraction. "Invade the area with space," he would counsel in his slow, heavily accented English.

EXPERIMENT *Sensing Space*

Set aside fifteen minutes. Sit comfortably and close your eyes, feeling your feet on the floor and the weight of your body as you sit. Take a few slow deep breaths and settle in.

Sense into the space in front of your body. Physical objects such as walls are no barrier. Imagine breathing into and out of this space. How far does it extend? Is there any limit?

Sense into the space behind your body. Breathe into and out of this space. Can you sense any limit?

Sense the space on the left side and then on the right.

Sense into the space above your body and then below.

Sense the space globally, all around you in every direction.

Now sense the space inside of your body. Is there any difference between the space inside and outside of your body?

Be all of this open space.

As you open your eyes, notice if you are able to retain this sense of space while sitting. Then notice how it is as you get up and move. ●

In time this sense of global space becomes a familiar friend and ally when exploring your inner experience.

Breathe into Your Experience

When my clients are encountering a difficult feeling or sensation, I often encourage them to gently breathe into it for a little while. The breath serves as a focus of attention. Gently focused breathing is a somatic form of listening.

EXPERIMENT *Breathing into a Contraction*

Sit comfortably, close your eyes, and sense into the interior of your body. Notice if there is an area of constriction or contraction, or any part that is calling for attention.

Gently and slowly breathe into this area, as if your inhalation and exhalation originate from here. For instance, if you sense heaviness or constriction in the solar plexus or the heart area, simply imagine that you are able to directly breathe into and out of this area.

Let your breath gently go into the center of the contraction. Feel your way into the core of it and continue to gently breathe for a minute or two. ●

The point of breathing into a feeling or sensation is not to change it but to become more intimate with it. Often we can sense a slight shift or release of an area that we have touched in this way. Something inside melts a little. Other feelings, thoughts, images, or memories may spontaneously arise. If this happens, it is enough to simply take note. Sometimes it can be quite surprising what we find in the core of a contraction. If we go deeply enough, we will always find space.

It is important that we not dig or troll for difficult experiences. Doing so is a form of subtle grasping in service to the endless self-improvement project. It is enough to be with discomfort as it arises. We don't need to go looking for it; if it needs attention, it will find us. I have an informal "three knocks on the door" rule for attending to my emotional and somatic experience. If something keeps asking for my attention, I give it. Otherwise, I let it go. If it is important, I know that it will be back.

Feel Your Feelings, Sense Your Sensations

Are you willing to allow your experience to be as it is, no matter what? What if this difficult feeling—shame, guilt, rage, terror—were to always be here? This question checks whether your acceptance comes with conditions. It is important that you are willing for your experience to never change. The point of this approach is not to change your experience but rather to be intimate with it. The apparent paradox is that when you are not fixated on a goal to change yourself, change naturally happens.

Be willing to feel your feelings fully as they are. If there is grief, allow the upwelling of sadness. If there is anger, allow the heat of it to flare up. If there is shame, allow the wave of it to wash through you. If there is terror, let yourself tremble and shake. This does not mean that you should act out these feelings. Learn how to tolerate them instead.

Be willing to sense your sensations as well. Become acquainted with the interior of your body and the shifting texture of sensations, particularly in the heart area and the gut. Open to sensing areas of numbness, constriction, or intensity. Explore the texture and shape of them.

Question Your Beliefs

Be willing to uncover and question all of your cherished beliefs, particularly your limiting self-judgments. I will thoroughly explore this step in the next chapter.

Be the Experience

Ultimately we are not separate from any so-called inner or outer experience. We are all of it even as we are a highly individuated being. We are both undivided being and a unique being—quite the paradox for the mind. Usually we approach our experience from the standpoint of a separate self: "I am someone, an apparent subject, who is experiencing an object such as a tormenting thought, an intense feeling, or uncomfortable sensation." It is one thing to be close to our experience in the moment. It is another to close the gap entirely and actually be the experience without being fused or merged with it.

EXPERIMENT *Be the Experience*

Allow yourself to experience a difficult emotion when it arises—for example, shame, fear, loneliness, or anger.

Sense it in your body. Notice how and where it localizes.

Now simply be it. Be whatever it is that you are experiencing. What happens?

I once encouraged a client to simply be the emptiness that she was feeling in the core of her body. She was at first terrified to get close to it, afraid of becoming lost in the sense of lack from which she had run for much of her life. Yet when she plunged into emptiness and became it, it opened into an enormous space that reminded her of a light-plane flight she had once taken through the Grand Canyon.

In another case, I was helping one of my clients explore a deep feeling of loneliness. At one point she found herself terribly alone and bereft in the middle of an arid desert. There was desolation in every direction she looked. When I guided her to be the desert, her experience immediately transformed into a feeling of deep connection with all of life. She realized that her feeling of disconnection was a complete fabrication of her mind. While she did not have a partner at the time, she knew that she was unimaginably connected with the whole of life. After this revelation, her deep sense of loneliness never returned.

I worked with another client who found himself on a plateau facing a huge gorge that seemed impassable. The side he was standing on felt like his false self, which was concerned about how he appeared to others. He felt a deep yearning to make it to the other side, to what felt like his essential self. He was confused and in despair as to how it could ever happen. "Perhaps I will grow wings," he mused. I invited him to be the gorge. After a moment of initial confusion, he let himself simply be the immense chasm. He felt a huge relaxation in the core of his body and being—one of the key markers of the sense of inner knowing. There was nowhere to go and no chasm to cross. The image of the gorge was a mental construct. He was, to his great astonishment and relief, home.

Challenging Experiences:
Icy Places, Holes, and Floods

Clients sometimes encounter what seems like a frozen land undergoing an intense spring thaw, or they find what seem like gaping holes or intense floods. At some time, perhaps, we have felt deeply frozen, terrified to explore an apparently bottomless emotion like grief, or overwhelmed by intense feelings and sensations. For example, some years ago when I was no longer able to defend against a visceral fear of abandonment, my whole body shook uncontrollably for almost an hour.

The process of opening up is not always so dramatic. The intensity of our reactions depends upon the density of our conditioning. Sometimes we can make the entire journey on our own. Other times, particularly at critical junctures, it is very helpful to have an experienced guide alongside us. Her or his support and guidance can make the trip much more smooth and direct. The best guide is our inner knowing, and the best outer guides are in touch with this guidance within themselves.

Icy Places

Earlier in this chapter I wrote that one of the primary ways we defend ourselves is to freeze. Sometimes we fight, sometimes we flee, yet I suspect most often we freeze. We can encounter inner icy places at any level. Sometimes it can feel like the very core of our body is frozen. The beautiful thing about icy places is that they can always thaw. Global warming takes on a completely different meaning when we are talking about inner transformation and integration. One of my clients, David, whom you met at the beginning of chapter 1, gratefully reported that it felt like his inner Arctic was gradually melting.

Warming the interior of the body with our own affectionate attention leads to greater fluidity and aliveness. Sometimes it can be helpful to first find an area in our bodies that feels spacious and alive and then bring attention to an area or level that feels numb. Sharing a frozen area with someone trustworthy—a partner, friend, or therapist—can also quicken the thawing process, since so much of our inner ice originates from disrupted or absent relationships.

Holes

It is very common for people who are doing inner work to encounter what subjectively feels like a hole. I have found that these holes tend to localize around the major energy centers (see chapter 2), although this is not always the case. A hole is an area of deficiency. For instance, a hole in the heart center may correspond with a lack of self-love and self-acceptance.[3]

The absence of an essential quality, such as love, results in a felt sense of lack or deficiency. As I mentioned earlier in this chapter, we can defend our sensitivity so well that we lose touch with what we were defending. We can armor our heart or gut so thoroughly that we lose all feeling. Metaphorically speaking, an apparently empty hole is the entrance to an inner spring.

If we go deeply enough into a hole, in addition to discovering our natural wholeness, we may discover an essential quality. This was the case with my client who wanted to fly over the chasm. At the beginning of our session, he had reported feeling irreparably damaged by childhood abuse. When he fully opened to the chasm within himself and rested as it, he saw that there was no essential damage. "That was only on the surface," he calmly reported. In addition to knowing that he was whole, he discovered an essential quality of strength within himself.

Exploring the felt sense of a hole is a bit like underwater caving. We tend to avoid these zones of apparent lack out of fear of drowning in them. We may have fallen into a painful state of depression, anxiety, or grief in the past and struggled to pull ourselves out, like a gasping swimmer dragging himself onto the shore. Why, we might wonder, would we ever willingly go there again? If we are interested in authenticity, we will be compelled to go. Yet it is important that we have enough inner resilience and outer support to reenter a hole without becoming overwhelmed and lost in it. If we are going to dive underwater again, we will need the equivalent of good scuba gear, a strong light, an accurate map, and usually an experienced diving buddy if the hole is particularly deep. While it is possible to do this kind of exploration alone, it is sometimes safer and easier to do it with support.

Floods

A flood corresponds to a feeling of being emotionally or energetically overwhelmed. Stepping into a hole without sufficient resources can lead to flooding and retraumatization. Peter Levine, PhD, the originator and developer of Somatic Experiencing, has described the phenomenon of the "trauma vortex," where we can get overwhelmed much like someone gets sucked down into a whirlpool.[4] This can happen when we reexperience a prior trauma and become so overwhelmed by it that the original traumatic pattern is actually reinforced. To avoid retraumatizing his clients, Levine developed a specialized approach that involves gradually shifting attention back and forth (pendulating) between a state of calm stability and states of chaos associated with the original trauma, and doing so in small doses (titrating). This approach allows the body-mind to more easily integrate the original trauma without being overwhelmed.

Single-incident traumas, such as a one-time beating or serious accident, can often be quickly resolved with a few sessions of EMDR

(Eye Movement Desensitization and Reprocessing).[5] Chronic trauma, particularly at the hands of an early caretaker, is usually much more complex and time-consuming to resolve.

The psyche is surprisingly resilient. Sometimes a flood of overwhelming feeling and sensation can spontaneously resolve without specialized methods or helpers. It is important to keep an open mind about the possibility for spontaneous healing. On the other hand, it is equally important to recognize that certain conditions of chronic trauma usually require specialized care. While you can learn ways to tap into and build your resilience, professional help is sometimes essential.[6]

Summary

While our psychological conditioning makes it harder to attune with our inner knowing, it also can be a portal to our depths if it is approached with the right quality of attention and understanding. Apparent obstacles such as turbulent emotions and bodily constrictions can become allies pointing the way to treasures that have been buried and forgotten deep within. Accepting and exploring our defenses and their effects—our inner icy places, holes, and occasional floods—will eventually lead us to our natural sensitivity and inner strength. Every challenging inner experience bears a hidden gift.

Our suffering is a wake-up call prompting us to become intimate with our experience just as it is. While the conditioned mind can accept conditionally, only our true nature accepts unconditionally. Learning to recognize and rest in and as the background awareness behind all thoughts, feelings, and sensations brings a sense of inner freedom, space, and intimacy with whatever we experience. It is our greatest inner resource.

Resolving certain challenging experiences, particularly those that originate from trauma or serious disruptions in early emotional bonding, may require the help of mental health professionals who are trained to deal with these complex psychological states and issues. And sometimes these issues can resolve themselves. See how far you can get on your own, and if you need help, don't be afraid to ask for it.

4

questioning core beliefs, dialoguing with the inner critic, and witnessing thoughts

The primary task of any good spiritual teaching is not to answer your questions, but to question your answers.

ADYASHANTI

For years Debra struggled with a complicated and mysterious illness that severely restricted what she could eat. After seeing many doctors and healers, she had not found an effective treatment. Her illness left her exhausted and anxious about the troubling side effects of her extremely meager and imbalanced diet. Because she could neither eat normally nor easily explain her condition to others, she became socially isolated as well. As stressful as her condition was, the hardest part for her was dealing with her self-judgments. When she first came to see me, she tormented herself with the belief that she was to blame for her illness and her inability to heal it, even though she suspected that this was not rational. She felt a profound sense of shame.

Taking a family history and following her feelings back in time, we discovered that this shame originated in her early childhood. When her mother died, Debra was taken in and raised by relatives who treated her like an unwanted burden. As a result, she learned to be as invisible as possible, making few demands and feeling apologetic for her very existence. Her self-view and worldview took form: she believed and felt that she was an unwanted and unlovable orphan in an abandoning and unwelcoming world. Her current health struggles were triggering this deeply held view from her childhood.

Much of our work together centered around recognizing and seeing through these early and extremely influential beliefs. We sat quietly together, welcomed the feeling of deep shame, and then investigated the layers of belief that gave rise to it, such as: "I don't deserve to exist. I am without value. My needs and feelings are unimportant. I am a burden on others, and I am responsible for bad things that happen" (such as her mother's death and her own illness). As she sorted through these beliefs, I encouraged Debra to ask herself, "What is the truth? What is my deepest knowing about this?"

Over time, Debra's self-judgments and shame gradually lessened. She was increasingly able to see her beliefs as beliefs rather than as the truth. She experienced a growing sense of space around her thoughts and discovered how linked her thoughts and feelings actually were. She also could see how she had clung to these beliefs about herself in order to remain within a familiar identity. As the grip on her old self-image loosened, she began to experience a growing sense of inner peace and silence. Her search for healing continued, but was less burdened by self-judgment and shame. She stopped second-guessing herself and accepted that she was doing the best that she could with a very challenging situation.

It was striking for me to discover that Debra's greatest suffering came from her self-judgments rather than her extreme health challenge. She certainly felt an ongoing fear and despair about her fragile health, but her underlying beliefs and feelings about the apparent meaning of her condition were far more distressing.

In chapter 3, I touched upon the critical role that our beliefs play in terms of how we feel, sense, and act. They are often hidden or only vaguely in our conscious awareness, yet they are at the root of the majority of our reactive feelings and bodily contractions. As important as it is to be willing to feel our feelings and sense our sensations, it is equally important that we uncover and see through our core limiting beliefs. To do so, we have to inquire deeply. Until we do, our old reactive patterns will continue to dominate us like noisy children grabbing the steering wheel. There will be too much static in the system to hear the quieter signal of our inner knowing.

Identifying Core Limiting Beliefs

Core limiting beliefs are always very simple. This is not surprising since they usually form during childhood. They will reflect a child's view even if they are couched in sophisticated language. They can usually be summarized in short declarative statements of seven words or less. The most powerful ones are almost always about ourselves.

The grandmother and grandfather of all core limiting beliefs are "I am not enough" and "Something is wrong with me." All other limiting beliefs can trace their origins back to one or both of these two. As long as we maintain a separate sense of self, we will carry some degree of the belief that we are lacking or flawed. It is the inevitable baggage of the "little me."

The first step in questioning our core beliefs is to be able to recognize them. There are three main ways to detect them:

1. Ask yourself

2. Sense your body

3. Observe your judgments of others

Ask Yourself

This is the direct method of inquiry. When I occasionally ask my clients, "What do you imagine is wrong with you?" I am always struck by how much this simple question evokes. They usually have a list of self-judgments. If it is a long list, I may write down their beliefs and then ask which of them is most loaded. I help them to find the one that has the most juice and distill it so that its impact can be felt and sensed in the body. It is always best to find your own formulation; the wording is important. For instance, "I am really screwed up" may have much more impact to you than "Something is wrong with me."

EXPERIMENT   *Sensing the Impact of Limiting Beliefs*

Write down a short list of what you think is lacking or wrong with you. Keep the sentences very brief.

When you are done, find the one that has the most charge. Refine it so that it says exactly what you think. Take a minute to give your attention to it. Notice how it impacts your feelings and sensations in the interior of your body.

Then take a deep breath and let it go. •

Sense Your Body

Your body responds immediately to your thoughts. A limiting belief will always create a reactive feeling and constrictive sensation, as you may have noticed doing the above experiment. It is very important to see this link. Sensing your body is another easy way to detect your core limiting beliefs. I usually invite my clients to feel their feelings and sense their sensations before examining their underlying beliefs. This keeps the inquiry grounded in the body and allows them to feel the inner shift and release when a belief is seen through. You don't need to go looking for inner constrictions. It is enough to note them when they arise.

EXPERIMENT   *Uncovering Beliefs through Somatic and Emotional Reactions*

Whenever you notice an inner constriction or emotional reaction in your body, slow down, breathe, and sense into it. Give it lots of space and be willing to feel into it.

After a minute or two, ask yourself, "What is the belief about myself that goes with this constriction or reaction?" Take your time to find the right wording. ●

Observe Your Judgments of Others

Our self-judgments are hidden within our most frequent and charged judgments of others. It's called projection: we throw out or project onto others what we are unaware of in ourselves. The more that we cannot stand something in ourselves, the more vigorously we project it onto others. On the other hand, the more self-aware we are, the less we project onto and judge others. For example, I used to be very judgmental of others' anger until I realized that I had repressed anger within myself. As I made friends with my anger, which took a while, I became much more comfortable with it in others. It no longer threatened me. In psychological terms, I had owned my anger, although no one actually owns anything. It was simply a matter of being conscious of what was happening.

In time we may realize that we have done or could do anything that we judge others for doing. While we may never act on these impulses, we can certainly find them in our thoughts, feelings, and dreams. I can recall feeling a surprising sense of relief some years ago when I acknowledged that I was capable of murderous rage. I saw that I was no different or better than the rest of humanity. All human tendencies, angelic or demonic, are within us.

EXPERIMENT *Recognizing Projections*

Think of some quality or behavior that you just cannot stand in others, such as cruelty, selfishness, dishonesty, disloyalty, greed, weakness, vanity, arrogance, or rage.

Bring to mind the image of someone who appears to have these qualities. What is your judgment about him or her?

Then take a few minutes to see if you can find these qualities within yourself. What is your judgment about these qualities within yourself? ●

Questioning Core Limiting Beliefs

Once we have successfully identified our core limiting beliefs, it is important to deeply question them. There are some useful formal ways to do this, such as "The Work" of Byron Katie or the Sedona Method.[1] Sometimes it is sufficient to simply recognize our limiting beliefs. Bringing them into the daylight of conscious awareness may be enough to dispel them, like a morning sun that burns off a light fog. Usually, however, it takes more time and attention. The cloud covering of our beliefs is often quite thick.

We tend to be attached to our beliefs since they define who we think we are. Losing them can be both liberating and deeply unsettling. I have always been struck by how important what we believe is to religious people. "Do you believe in God?" never struck me as the right question. Inquiring into who or what is aware of a belief is much more fruitful!

If you are going to question your beliefs, it is important that you really want to know the truth. This may not always be the case; often we are more interested in safety, comfort, or pleasure. Your willingness to explore will directly impact the depth of your discovery. Your inquiry is most potent when it is full-hearted. As you enter this self-investigation, it is important to ask yourself how much you are interested in the truth and to be honest about your answer. Deep inquiry strips away layers of falsehood. You may not want to be so naked.

If our inquiry stays on the level of the mind, it has limited impact. For example, cognitive therapy engages the rational mind to challenge irrational beliefs. This can offer a certain level of relief; however, how often have you thought, "I know this doesn't make any rational sense, but I still feel this way"? I hear this from my clients all the time. It is as if our adult self already knows better, but there is an inner child who remains unconvinced. There is a good reason for this.

As I mentioned earlier, almost all of our core limiting beliefs originate in childhood. Based upon very limited information, resources, and understanding, these simple beliefs are emotionally charged and deeply embedded in the body. They are largely subconscious or unconscious. As a result, they do not easily yield to rational analysis. They have to be approached with something other than our rational thinking in order to be seen through fully.

Fortunately, our inner knowing, our heart wisdom, is able to penetrate this level of conditioning. Over the years of working with clients, I have found that if people bring attention to the heart center, get quiet, and consult their deepest inner knowing, a powerful transformative wisdom will arise. Based upon this discovery, I have created the following simple method for questioning limiting beliefs.

EXPERIMENT *Inquiry into Core Limiting Beliefs*

1. **Notice a distressing feeling or sensation in your body.**
   Take a minute to feel or sense it more fully. (If you already
   know one of your core limiting beliefs, take a few minutes
   to sense the impact in your body and then skip to step 3.)

2. **Ask yourself: "What is the belief that goes with this
   feeling or sensation?"** Focus on limiting beliefs about
   yourself. A limiting belief about others or the world will
   almost always have a corresponding belief about yourself.
   Example: "The world is dangerous and overwhelming"
   corresponds to "I can't handle it." Keep the belief as
   brief as possible. Four to seven words are usually enough.
   Check for resonance. Does the belief strongly correspond
   with the feeling or sensation? Choose the phrase that has
   the most charge. Write it down, if you need to. Examples:
   "I am not enough"; "I am deeply flawed."

3. **Bring your attention to the heart area, in the center of
   your chest, and ask, "What is the truth? What is my
   deepest knowing about this?"** Let the question go, be
   quiet, then listen, sense, and feel what comes. Don't go
   to your mind for an answer. The response may or may
   not be verbal. It may come as a feeling, sensation, image,

or a direct knowing. There may be different responses for different levels of experience. A statement might be untrue on one level and true on another. For example, the belief that "I am not enough" may be relatively untrue yet ultimately true. Take your time with this step.

4. **Let the response/answer saturate your body. Breathe it in. Feel the impact in your body.** It is important to take a few minutes to do this, because it allows the body and mind to absorb and integrate the insight and to establish new neural, cognitive, emotional, and energetic networks.

5. **Revisit your original limiting belief. How does it strike you now?** Usually the charge will be gone or greatly diminished, and the thought will seem either false or irrelevant. You may discover a different or related belief that is charged. If this is the case, continue your inquiry into it.

Members of my self-inquiry groups have recently been exploring this method. One woman groaned as she confessed the core belief "I am unlovable." With dread and shame she had named her greatest demon. Yet when she brought her attention to her heart center and innocently inquired into the truth, there was an immediate and unexpected nonverbal response: a tremendous upwelling of love for herself. She opened her arms out toward the other group members as if radiating a great light. It was almost too much for her to let in. I encouraged her to slow down, to breathe, and to absorb this love. Even though the original message of being unlovable had been overtly and covertly hammered into her as a little girl, her heart knew otherwise.

Another member went through a quick mental list of all of his apparent deficiencies and settled on the classic "I am not enough." When he consulted his heart, he got a surprising response: as long as he took himself as a separate self, he would always feel that he was not enough, no matter what he did. He saw that the sense of lack came from defining himself by some story. He then sensed the fullness that came when he allowed himself to be undefined. There was no longer even a question of being or not being enough. The rational mind can never spontaneously produce this kind of existential insight.

One of my clients, who periodically struggles with overeating, took this struggle as evidence that something was terribly wrong with her. When she checked in with her heart wisdom, she felt a palpable sense of relief as she discovered that this belief was untrue. Her direct knowing was not an affirmation or psychological reframing of her issue, nor did it deny the reality of her struggle. It simply acknowledged that her core story was untrue: there was nothing fundamentally wrong with her, no matter what. This intuitive realization brings great freedom.

The Art of Sitting with a Question

The mind likes a simple yes or no, yet life presents itself in endless shades of gray. A creative response will be nuanced and unique for each situation. If we are unsure of our next step or puzzled by something, it is good to slow down and check inside for guidance. I have learned that there is an art to sitting with a question that catalyzes the emergence of a deeper intelligence.

The first step is to clarify the question. What are you really asking? Take time to make it as clear as possible. Once you have formulated it, pose it to yourself and then be quiet, as I suggest in step 3 of the earlier inquiry method. It is like dropping a stone into a pond—toss it in and then watch the ripples. Don't look to your thinking mind for an answer. This is not an analytic process. Let your attention rest in your heart center. A response can come from any direction—a felt sense, a waking or dream image, an emotion, or a direct knowing. If the response feels resonant, act on it and see how it works out.

The Inner Critic

We have an inner critic—that part of the mind that creates an idea of how we and the world should be. The critic is actually a mental process, rather than a discrete entity. This inner critic is never satisfied; no matter how we or the world are, it is never good enough. When political and religious ideologues assume positions of power and try to impose their ideals, they bring great suffering to their subjects. Pol Pot, the idealistic communist leader who transformed the former Cambodia into a killing field in the 1980s, is a good example. Similarly, when we give the inner critic authority by believing it, we create a kind of inner killing field that chokes off any spontaneity and self-trust.

You can easily detect the presence of this kind of tyrannical thinking within yourself: just notice when you have a thought that includes "should" or "should not." How often do you torment yourself by thinking, "I should not be experiencing this" or "This should or should not be happening" or "He or she should or should not be doing that." If you observe your thinking for a few minutes, you will usually find evidence of this critical tendency. It is pervasive and persuasive.

Judging always creates distance within yourself and between yourself and others. I can recall the relief I felt as I gradually discovered the difference between how I thought I should be versus how I actually was, between an ideal and the real. If you relate to your experience as you think it should be, you keep it at arm's length. For example, if you believe that you should not be experiencing a difficult feeling such as anger, shame, or fear, you will not give your full affectionate attention to it. You will ignore it, push it away, or try to change it.

The same process of refusal applies to others. If you believe that others should not be as they are, you will also try to ignore them, keep them at a distance, or change them. On the other hand, if you approach your life with the question, "What *is* actually happening?" you will have a very different experience. Judging always creates alienation. Nonjudgmental, affectionate attention fosters intimacy and understanding.

Judging is different from discerning. Judging is about determining what is right or wrong, good or bad. Discerning is about clear seeing. Letting go of our judgments does not mean that we lose discernment. In fact, judging is a distortion of discernment. Once we are able to see through the mind's tendency to judge everything dualistically, in terms of good and bad and right and wrong, we are actually much freer to see things as they are and respond appropriately. On a social level, thieves and murderers will still need to be isolated from the rest of society until they change their attitudes and behaviors. On an individual level, we may no longer want to spend time with someone, yet we can do so without closing our heart and condemning him or her. We can set clear boundaries *and* keep our hearts open.

It has been a surprising discovery in my work with clients that the inner critic almost always means well. Strange as it may seem, even as the judging mind may torment us, it is full of good intentions. It is not the enemy; it is innocently confused.

Sometimes in my work with clients I will ask to speak directly to their inner critics. People who are heavily burdened with self-criticism are usually strongly identified with this inner voice and have difficulty stepping back from it. If we can first step into this self-critical voice without judging it and explore its origins and intentions, and then step back and witness it from a place of compassion, the experience can be revelatory. When I talk to these inner critics directly, I discover that they are always trying to help my clients, albeit unskillfully. For instance, they may believe that harsh criticism will lead to self-improvement and eventual approval by others. Or they may believe that it is less painful to stick the knife of self-criticism into themselves than to have it done by another—a compassionate preemptive self-strike. Reflexive self-apology, where we automatically apologize for whatever we do, is one form of this. Inner critics may also be attached to a pattern of self-criticism as a way to stay connected to one of their critical parents or as a way to avoid the uncertainty of not knowing.

While the inner judge may at first appear to be as authoritative as a Supreme Court justice, in fact it is more like the "great and powerful" Wizard of Oz. "Pay no attention to the man behind the curtain," commands the voice of the wizard as Dorothy's dog, Toto, pulls away the veil. The source of the booming voice is an ordinary man with a microphone and no real authority. This seemingly authoritative voice of judgment actually forms in childhood. In essence, it is a child dressed up as an adult. It is doing the best it can with limited resources and understanding to guide us to survive and navigate life with as little pain as possible. It is using an innate adaptive strategy of the mind that exists in all people of all cultures. We pay a heavy price when we believe what it tells us.

Certainly the inner critic can be deeply influenced by our parents and educators. We internalize their critical voices and then add our own layers of self-critique onto them. Even a relatively benign psychological upbringing will not prevent this self-critical tendency, which seems to grow out of the ground on its own. This is particularly evident in early adolescence, when the critical mind easily finds fault with everyone and everything. You may have gone through this phase when you were a teenager or when you raised one.

I don't try to reform the views of these inner critics when I dialogue with them. It is usually enough for them to step forward without condemnation and tell their stories. They discover things about themselves, and they also learn about the effects of their criticism. The critical and criticized parts overhear each other as each comes out of the shadows, takes the center stage of attention, and has a turn to speak. It is an inner truth and reconciliation process.

When these voices are witnessed with compassionate clarity, they have a way of gradually harmonizing. No part needs to leave; each holds a valuable quality, even if it is initially masked. For example, the inner critic expresses the essential quality of discernment in a distorted form. Its true nature is to see clearly rather than to judge. A judged part usually carries some early unexpressed human need. For example, one of my clients recently discovered that the root of his sexual acting out came from a deep childhood need to be held and soothed by a nurturing maternal energy.

You can have a dialogue with your own inner critic in writing or out loud. You may find a friend or partner to help you, or you can do it on your own. This approach is strongly influenced by Voice Dialogue, a method developed by Hal and Sidra Stone which grew out of Gestalt therapy.[2]

EXPERIMENT *Dialoguing with the Inner Critic*

Invite your inner critic to come forward. Then become it. Take your time and get a feel for the energy and physical posture that goes with this voice. It can be helpful to get out of your seat and stand, move about, or take another physical position.

As the critic, write or speak about how long you have been around, where you learned what you did, what your intentions are, what you need, how you feel, and how well your criticisms appear to work.

When you have finished, shift gears, and take the voice and posture of the part of you that feels criticized. As this part, express your experience of how long you have felt criticized, how you feel, what you need, and what the effects of the criticism have been.

Go back and forth between the voices, taking turns writing or speaking as each of them, until you feel complete. They don't need to agree with each other. It is enough that each honestly speaks and listens.

Stand back from both voices and assume the voice of a compassionate witness. Observe what has been expressed without judgment. Notice the relationship between the critic and the criticized.

Take your original sitting position and notice how you feel in your body. How and where do you experience each of the voices in your body?

What is the overall impact of this experiment? ●

Witnessing Thoughts

Some years ago I had the good fortune to befriend Suzanne Segal, a delightful psychologist based in the Bay Area who had experienced a deep opening of awareness several years before we met.[3] A year before she died from a brain tumor, she gathered around her a group of friends whom she called her "playmates in the vastness." Sometimes she would invite us to "see thoughts as thoughts." At first this was a puzzling instruction for me; it seemed so obvious—of course thoughts are thoughts. In time I realized the importance of this simple invitation. To see thoughts *as* thoughts means to see that they are not reality; they are maps of reality. Some maps are more accurate than others, yet none are reality itself. It also means to see thoughts as objects in awareness, rather than awareness itself. It was her way of describing the witnessing of thought.

To witness something means to see it clearly, without judgment, as a scientist would during an experiment. If you are a marine biologist observing the habits of a rare sea cucumber or a physicist at CERN (the European Center for Nuclear Research) observing possible evidence of the Higgs particle, you will want to see things as they actually are, not as you want or expect them to be. Similarly, it is very liberating to witness your thoughts without judgment and without any agenda to change or get rid of them.

Some meditative practices try to quiet the mind and even stop the process of thought through concentrating on a particular object, such as the breath or a mantra. In fact, thinking can be quieted and even briefly stopped during meditation; however, it always reappears. There is a humorous teaching story about a highly accomplished yogi who asked his student to get him a glass of water. Before the student could return with the water, the yogi slipped into a thought-free *samadhi* that lasted for days. When the yogi finally came out, the first thing he said was, "Where's my water?" Desire and fear will continue even if thoughts temporarily stop. It is the nature of the mind to think as long as we are alive. An overly constrained mind becomes dull.

As we begin to observe our thoughts, we will discover that they conform to certain familiar patterns. Many of them are about things that we think we need to do—our inner to-do list. The first thoughts upon waking are usually "What day is this, and what do I have to do?" This is the completely normal function of the mind that is concerned with orienting in time and planning for the apparent future. This mental tendency is not a problem, just something to be observed.

Sometimes thoughts are about what has already happened—the apparent past. In this case, we may be savoring an experience or trying to make sense of it. In both cases, attention shuttles between the apparent past and future. I say "apparent" because the past and the future exist only in our minds. If we take a moment to observe our actual experience, we will discover that it is only happening right now, including memory of the so-called past and imagination of the so-called future. See if this is true in your own experience.

Contemplating "right now" is an intriguing experience. When exactly is it? As soon as we think about it, it has already passed. When we try to look for "now," we discover that it is also an idea. "Now" does not exist on some time line between the past and future. This contemplation, a classic one in some meditative traditions, can catapult attention into timeless awareness. Sometimes it will happen spontaneously. I first had this realization one afternoon when I was twenty-one; I briefly saw that everything is happening during a now that it is not localized in time. This insight was hard to put into words, but the impact was palpable. A veil briefly lifted, allowing for a "peek" experience.

Many of our thoughts are arguments with reality—judgments that something should or should not be happening. Have you noticed that reality never conforms to an ideal? Often these arguments are with other people. We usually don't argue with the weather; we see how it is and adjust to it. If it is raining, we take an umbrella. If it is cold, we put on a coat. On the other hand, we tend to inwardly argue with people at great length, particularly if we feel hurt or misunderstood. It is fascinating to see all of the judgments of others that arise during these inner arguments. As we saw earlier in this chapter, it is freeing to withdraw these projections and see how they may apply to ourselves.

Thinking is associative; one thought will lead to another in a train of thought. It is useful to observe this associative process and see how easily attention unknowingly boards this train. As soon as we see it, our attention is off the train—it spontaneously disembarks. Daydreaming is a form of inner train-hopping.

Most of our thinking is repetitive. It is as if attention follows a familiar groove, like a needle on a vinyl record. There are almost certainly neurological correlates—networks of synapses that correspond to these habitual thought patterns. Occasionally our thinking is new and creative. We make new connections, learn new things, and are sometimes inspired by what feels like a higher source. Some of the greatest scientists and artists, including Albert Einstein, Johannes Brahms, and Rumi, have described this process of receiving spontaneous insights through words, images, symbols, or sounds.

Awareness: The Witnessing of Thoughts

So far I have been describing different kinds of thoughts. But what is it that is aware of thought? What is it that is witnessing? Something is aware of thought that is not itself a thought. Some call it awareness; others call it bare attention. The name is not important. When attention, either purposefully or spontaneously, turns away or steps back from thoughts, it relaxes into its source.

Attention is like a wave of awareness. It arises to focus on a thought, feeling, or sensation and then resolves back into an open state, much as a wave subsides into the ocean. Attention has also been compared to the lens of a camera that can focus when needed on an object and then defocus back to a panoramic overview. At some point, as you simply notice thoughts, allow your attention to shift to that which is noticing. What is the nature of this awareness?

EXPERIMENT *Being Awareness*

Sit comfortably, close your eyes, take a few deep breaths, and settle in. Notice your present experience. Feel the various sensations of your body—touch, sound, taste, and smell. Take your time to observe each of these.

Bring your attention to any emotions you may be experiencing. Notice how they feel in the interior of your body.

Be aware of the thoughts that arise and pass through your mind like clouds that come and go in the sky. Don't try to stop or change them. Notice when your attention hops onto a train of thought.

Ask yourself, "What is this that is aware of thought?" Don't think about it. Relax into this background awareness.

Notice the nature of this awareness. Does it exist at any time other than now? Can it be located in space? Does it have any center or boundary? Does it have any form at all? Explore your experience of it.

Can this awareness be defined, or is it empty of all definitions? Does it refuse anything, or is it open to all experience? Is it unconscious, or is it awake, aware, and knowing?

Now *be* this empty, open, awake awareness. ●

It generally takes time to discern thought from awareness since we are so identified with thinking. The mind tends to dismiss silent openness as an absence of something, since awareness is not an object. With some attention, however, this background awareness comes more into the foreground. We can't force this way of seeing.

One of the subtle traps of observing thought is to take on the role of being a separate witness. I remember an early talk I attended with Jean Klein when he was describing the quality of openness that was inherent in pure listening. I asked him about being a witness to thought, and he responded, "Don't fornicate with the witness!" With this colorful phrase, he was strongly warning me to not become attached to an identity as a separate witness. This is a common dead end for long-term meditators; they are able to watch their thoughts, feelings, and sensations and yet still retain a sense of being a subtly separate observer. This was true of me after fifteen years of regular meditation. Jean could sense this fixation in my attention. Even as witnessing happens, there is no separate witness.

Attention may move back and forth between the foreground of thoughts and the background of unbounded awareness for some time. At first, experiencing this background can feel like visiting a very restful getaway. We may briefly touch this quiet openness for a few minutes and then return to our busy lives. It can feel like renting a beautiful vacation house for a week and then returning home for the rest of the year. At some point there is a shift of identity, and we realize that the vacation rental is our true home and what we thought was our home—our conventional identity as a separate being bounded by space and time—is the temporary rental unit. This happens when we are deeply convinced that our true nature is infinite, empty, open, wakeful awareness. The trance of identifying with thought lifts, and an awakening *from* the mind occurs. This critically important step brings a sense of great peace and freedom. It is a tremendous relief to realize that we are not confined by any story. It is the beginning of a new way of life.

A common pitfall with this initial awakening is to take it on as a new identity: "I am the awake one." In this case, we now have a new story of being a special someone—someone who knows that he or she is no one! The illusion of separation continues in a subtler form if we identify with this view. It is important to recognize this identification, see through it, and continue in our inquiry into the nature of reality.

Summary

Confusing thought with reality is the greatest obstacle to discovering and nurturing our sense of inner knowing. In this chapter I introduced three ways of approaching our thoughts that can help free us from them:

1. Recognizing and questioning core limiting beliefs

2. Dialoguing with the inner critic

3. Witnessing thoughts *as* thoughts

Most of our reactive feelings and somatic constrictions originate from the core limiting beliefs that we hold. It is extremely useful to be able to recognize these core beliefs that originated in childhood and to question them from our deepest knowing. There is a simple and powerful way of doing so that invokes the wisdom of the heart.

The inner critic is that part of us that judges our experience based on an ideal. While this judgmental process is intended to be helpful, it always creates distance within ourselves and between ourselves and others. Judging is a distortion of an underlying capacity to discern—a capacity that we all possess. Dialoguing with the inner critic, along with the parts that are criticized, involves first stepping into a part of the self, expressing from it, and then stepping back and witnessing it with compassionate understanding. Accepting these parts as they are and giving them voice fosters a natural inner reconciliation.

Witnessing thoughts as thoughts means we recognize that thoughts are only maps of reality, not reality itself. Some thoughts are more accurate than others; however, none are ultimately true. Witnessing thoughts also means that we are able to distinguish thought from that which is aware of thought. As this happens, it is important not to become identified as being a separate witness. At some point we will no longer identify with our thoughts or as a separate witness. Instead, we will recognize our true nature as an open, empty, awake awareness.

PART III

hearing the signals:
somatic qualities of inner knowing

Recently, my wife and I took a hike in the high Sierras. The beginning of the route was not obvious, but as we gradually ascended the granite ridge, I began to notice small piles of stones, called cairns, marking the way.

The four bodily signals of inner knowing—relaxed groundedness, inner alignment, openheartedness, and spaciousness—are like these cairns. They are markers on the path, helping to validate and guide those of us who are learning to recognize and trust our inner knowing.

It is important to realize that these markers are not an end in themselves. The goal is not to collect bigger and better cairns. Rather, these markers lead us to something much more precious—our inner knowing. They are our body's way of telling us that we are on the right track.

While knowing is prior to any sensation, our body participates in this knowing in subtle and recognizable ways. Everyone is wired a little differently and will experience this bodily knowing uniquely. I will explore the qualities of relaxed groundedness, inner alignment, openheartedness, and spaciousness as if they are distinct. In fact, they are interrelated; they are facets of the same diamond of inner knowing. As you attune with your truth, you may notice one of them more often than another. Each is an equally valid pointer to who we really are.

5

relaxed groundedness

*Men are afraid to forget their minds, fearing to
fall through the Void with nothing to stay their fall.
They do not know that the Void is not really void,
but the realm of the real dharma.*

HUANG PO

Gini bustled into my office several minutes late, flushed and a bit over-whelmed. As she sat on the sofa, catching her breath, she said, "I have *got* to get a grip on myself!"

"Maybe it's not so much about getting a grip as it is about letting it go," I suggested.

Gini was surprised by my response. She slowed down and looked at me more carefully; she was receptive and curious. As we quietly gazed for a minute or two, she relaxed and her attention clarified. Her breath slowed and her shoulders relaxed. Her eyes became calm, deep pools. Our attention dropped down from our heads into our bodies, like two passengers descending in an elevator.

Her tight inner grip quickly released, and we settled down into a deep, shared silence. We could both sense when she landed in her inner knowing; there is a palpable, spacious presence. The conversa-tion unfolded from this grounded clarity as Gini explored her desire to set boundaries with various family members and to answer a strong inner call to resume writing poetry.

Gini's story illustrates one of the most common markers of inner knowing: a core relaxation and sense of grounding. These two qualities are intimately related. When we open to our truth, a relaxation occurs in the core of the body and attention drops down from the head, moves through the body, and grounds like a tree rooting deeply into the earth.

Core Relaxation

Most of us unknowingly go through life with a tight grip in our inner core. This inner psychological grip corresponds to an outer physiological one. The mind is designed to grasp ideas, and the hands and arms are made to grasp objects. Each form of grasping is an attempt to be in control. Grasping something like a branch was useful for our ancestors, enabling them to swing through the trees, escape predators, gather fruit, and eventually make spears to hunt. Grasping ideas of ourselves and the world—virtual models of reality—allows us to plan, which provides a sense of control, however illusory this control may be.

We like to know who we are, how things work, and what others expect of us. Like Gini, in times of stress we may believe that we need to get a stronger grip on ourselves. In truth, we need to relax it. Our main stress comes from being too tightly wound. When I explain this principle to clients, I will sometimes use the metaphor of driving a car: if our grip on the steering wheel is too tense, we become a less safe driver. We need to be both alert *and* relaxed to gracefully navigate the road, as well as our life. Once Gini became deeply relaxed and grounded, she was able to approach the immediate challenges of her life with unusual clarity. If you reflect on your own life, I expect that you will discover the same thing. Too much tension obscures our natural wisdom.

We usually are not aware of this tension until we experience its opposite—a deep relaxation. This grip involves more than our muscles, although it includes them. For example, we can feel it as a tension in our face, jaw, shoulders and chest, solar plexus, lower belly, and even in our hands and feet. As our attention deepens and refines, we can also sense it in the core of our body. In addition to tensing physically, we tighten emotionally and energetically. We hold in our tender feelings and energies as a way to protect what is most precious—what we take to be ourselves.

We try to hold ourselves up and in as a way to survive. We instinctively and reflexively pull our attention up from the physical ground and in from the exterior of the body in order to be safe. For example, we naturally tense when we are afraid of potential physical danger. We are physically wired to anticipate and avoid it. Consider how you subtly tighten up when you are about to cross a busy street and how you relax once you have crossed.

Our deeper tension, however, is chronic and psychological. We are conditioned to try to control how we appear to others. We want to maintain an acceptable image within our "tribe," whether that tribe is our immediate family, a circle of friends, or our larger community. When we scratch the surface of a well-educated modern human, we find a tribal member.[1] There is a biological fear behind this concern for self-image. Outcasts never fared well in tribal societies—shunning meant almost certain death. When I explore my clients' social anxieties around acceptance and approval, there is always an underlying fear of rejection. Once they uncover this layer, I will ask, "Then what will happen?" They inevitably discover a fear of being abandoned, becoming homeless, and eventually dying. In most cases a secure middle-class lifestyle does not seem to lessen this primal fear.

There are still subtler and more powerful fears around releasing the chronic inner grip upon ourselves: we may lose control, become disoriented, and not know who we are. Essentially, it is a fear of the unknown. We tend to choose a known suffering over an unknown freedom. If I am not a contracted, separate self, what am I? What will happen if this tight fist—this inner contraction that relates to my core sense of self—lets go? Will I fragment and go insane? Will I be able to function in daily life? Will I disappear?

EXPERIMENT   *Inquiry into the Fear of Losing Your Grip*

What do you imagine would happen if you lost the inner grip on yourself? Ask yourself the question and then let it go.

Notice what comes up.

Bring your attention to your heart center and inquire: What is the truth? •

We are as afraid of living as we are of dying. Recently, a client described feeling a new type of anxiety arise as he stepped out more fully into the world as his authentic self. He had been badly abused and neglected growing up and had dissociated from his body and distanced himself from people as a way to survive. As a child, he had formed a relationship with an inner "green man" that personified his essential self and provided him with a sense of connection to something greater. In trauma literature this figure is known as an ISH—an inner self-helper. As a boy, my client had been terrified that his abusers would come in the middle of the night and abduct his green man. As we explored his experience more deeply, he had an epiphany. "What could ever be taken from me now?" he asked. He saw that he had been trying to protect an essence that could never be taken or harmed; there was actually nothing inside to protect. He felt deeply relieved and much freer to open to life as it is.

Our limited sense of self is always insecure. The collection of images and stories, with their related feelings and memories, that we take to be the self is plagued by an inherent feeling of groundlessness. Everything that we identify with—our bodies, feelings, thoughts, roles, work, loved ones, and environment—changes. We accurately sense that the inner and outer rug could be pulled out at any moment.

I felt this most acutely after the death of my first wife, Linda, in 1989. The fabric of a normal, smoothly flowing life was ripped open, and I saw through the illusion of a steady world. I had intellectually known of impermanence before, but now I had the direct, heartbreaking experience of it. Only people who have lost a loved one can know what this is like. I also discovered how much I had relied on Linda to fill a sense of lack in myself. Her death touched my own fear of mortality, as well as an inner sense of groundlessness. The Buddhist philosopher and Zen priest David Loy describes this experience:

> If the self is a delusive construct, there is a subtle
> yet significant distinction between the fear of death
> and fear of the void: Our deepest anxiety is our own
> groundlessness, which we become aware of as a sense
> of lack that motivates our compulsive attempts to
> ground ourselves, in one way or another. . . . This
> ungroundedness is like a hole at the core of my being.[2]

It was a sobering realization to see that I had been using my relationship with Linda to try to fill a hole in myself. Her death sparked a more honest and direct exploration into an underlying feeling of lack and my avoidance of it. Unknowingly, I had been subtly deceiving myself.

Personal and Essential Authenticity

Tension is inevitable when we live a lie and try to appear different from how we actually are. We don't want to appear vulnerable or needy. We don't trust that we are fundamentally enough as we are, even with our struggles and shortcomings. We compensate outwardly by trying to do things that will prove our value to others. We also edit our self-image as we describe our life to ourselves and others—the image-maintenance project. Often this habit becomes so automatic that we are unaware of it. We unknowingly adopt a mask and mistake it for our real face, assuming that our chronically tense and armored body is natural. It is normal, perhaps, but not natural.

As I mentioned in chapter 2, deception is an evolutionary survival strategy used by all living organisms.[3] When we use it, however, we feel tense and split within ourselves. While a few people are capable of lying without any inner tension, most of us feel uncomfortable when we do. The more sensitive and open we are, the less tolerable this inner discord becomes. A heartfelt confession (not of sin, but of the truth) brings tremendous relief. In the end, it always feels better to come clean and be in our integrity, even when there are painful consequences. Doing so is a sign of maturity.

I see the power of this truth in my psychotherapy practice, where my clients have a safe space to unpack all of the elements of their lives that they are afraid to reveal to others. A well-trained and mature psychotherapist offers a clear and compassionate space for clients to be witnessed and supported as they step through their shame, doubt, and fear and come into their integrity. Friends and partners can serve the same function if they are sufficiently accepting. Above all, though, we need to be honest with ourselves—a very challenging practice!

EXPERIMENT *Contemplate Deception*

Take a few minutes and reflect upon times when you were purposefully deceptive.

What was your motive for withholding the truth?

How did it feel, particularly in the interior of your body?

If you eventually disclosed the truth, what did you experience?

We are complex multidimensional beings and are able to be authentic on some levels and not on others. For example, some people are personally authentic but not in integrity with their deepest nature. They are honest at work and in their personal lives but live with a feeling of groundlessness, disconnected from the whole of life. Others may intuit a genuine connection with life but struggle with honesty on a personal level, often because of early unmet emotional needs.

We can see this most dramatically with spiritual teachers who exploit their students for sex, money, or power. Sadly, this has become common in the West. This is an important area to explore for those of us—students or teachers—who are interested in an essential way of living, since it appears that knowing one's deepest nature does not immediately translate into being personally authentic. I had once thought that personal authenticity would automatically evolve as we contacted our inner being, but this doesn't appear to be true. For personal authenticity to develop, there also needs to be a deep commitment to actualizing the truth in daily life. In addition to knowing our true nature, we also need to be honest and vulnerable on a human level.

As the degree of congruence between how we think, feel, and act grows, so does our experience of inner relaxation and aliveness. Personal authenticity—facilitated by being in touch with our underlying needs and feelings and being honest with others—allows us to feel more at ease in our own skin. We become more self-accepting and less defensive. However, a subtler and more profound level of relaxation occurs when we realize our essential authenticity as nonseparate, open, empty, awake awareness. When we are attuned and congruent with our deepest nature, the chronic inner grip of tension uncoils.

Trusting That We Are Held

One of the reasons that we try so hard to hold ourselves up and in is because we don't feel held by something greater. This brings us to the issue of trusting life, no matter what. Some call this trust *faith,* but faith usually means believing in something. Trust is not based on a belief. Rather, it is a felt sense of being held by a benevolent presence or field that is greater than the little me. Trust allows us to let go. This is not a trust that things will go as we want. Rather, it is a trust that life will unfold as it needs to.

Consider the following parable: Once there was a group of mountaineers who were trying to ascend K2, the second-highest peak in the world, in the Karakoram range in Pakistan. One night they were trapped in a terrible storm and were forced to turn back. During the perilous descent, one of the members lost his lighting, became separated from the group, and had to rappel the mountainside on his own. He came to the end of his rope, and he could not see or feel the ground beneath him. He was also too exhausted and cold to ascend. Hanging in the dark of the raging storm, he cried out for help, but no one could hear or see him. Although he was not a religious man, he calmed himself and prayed for guidance. The answer came immediately as a quiet inner voice, which said, "Just let go of the rope." He was too frightened to trust the guidance and continued to hold on. The following morning the search crew found him frozen to death, dangling in the air two feet above a rocky ledge.

Like the unfortunate mountaineer, we are frozen by our mistrust of life. We are reluctant to let go until we are completely certain that we are at the end of our metaphoric rope. Even then, we hold on. Often it takes a health or relationship crisis to catalyze a deep surrender of the illusion of control and a true willingness to let go.

When we feel held by something greater, however, it is much easier to trust and let go. Psychological conditioning can contribute to or detract from the sense of being held. If we have had a secure attachment with a caretaker and no major trauma growing up (see chapter 1), the sense of being held is easier to access and sustain. Yet this sense does not originate from or depend upon having been well parented. It is always available.

EXPERIMENT *Feeling Yourself Held by the Earth*

Find a comfortable chair in a quiet place and close your eyes. Take a few slow, deep breaths and relax.

Feel the weight of your body in the chair and the contact of your feet with the floor. Notice what it is like to allow your body to be held by the earth's gravity.

When you breathe, imagine your inhalation coming up from the earth and your exhalation releasing down into it. As your breath deepens into the earth, feel yourself completely held.

Relax into this sense. ◉

Sometimes I experience this sense of being held in nature. Whenever I close my eyes and float on my back in a lake or a bay, I spontaneously burst out laughing. The sense of being held by something greater, even on a physical level, is delightful. I highly recommend it! Denise Levertov captures the yearning for and effortless nature of this feeling in her poem "The Avowal":

> As swimmers dare
> to lie face to the sky

and water bears them,
as hawks rest upon air
and air sustains them
so would I learn to attain
freefall, and float
into Creator Spirit's deep embrace,
knowing no effort earns
that all-surrounding grace.

Levertov identifies a central paradox for the mind: letting go cannot be forced. The mind can relax, however, when it realizes that it does not know how to surrender.

My friend Steve Hadland, a hospice physician who lives by Tomales Bay on the California coast, experienced this sense of being deeply held while lying in his rowboat one clear, chilly morning in December.

The sun was well up and warmed my face as I rowed northwest into deeper waters. Apart from the sound of the oars and the splash of a seal, nothing broke the silence.

I slipped off the seat and lay back on the narrow deck looking up at the unclouded blue sky. Little waves lapped against the hull. Resting in the good company of sea, sun, and sky—this was what had been calling me. I felt soothed and rocked like a baby.

Recalling the words of the great sage Nisargadatta, "Pleasure and pain are only waves on an ocean of bliss," I allowed myself to feel not only the surface waves, but the palpable sense of being afloat, buoyed up by the bay and by the whole ocean itself—the vast, unbroken Pacific. The margins of body, boat, wave, and sea blurred and merged into one another. There was one boat, one sea, one world afloat in the black immensity of space, and I not apart from that.

The Four-Stage Continuum of Groundedness

The ground is both a metaphor and a felt sense. As a metaphor, it means to be in touch with reality. As a felt sense, it refers to feeling our center of gravity low in the belly and experiencing a deep silence, stability, and connection with the whole of life. Feeling grounded does not require contact with the earth; it can happen anywhere and anytime—even when we're flat on our backs in a rowboat.

Reality is inherently grounding. The more in touch with it we are, the more grounded we feel. This is as true of the facts of daily life as it is of our true nature. Life is multidimensional, ranging from the physical to the subtle to formless awareness. When we are in touch with physical reality, we feel physically grounded. As subtle levels of feeling and energy unfold, we feel subtly grounded. When we know ourselves as open awareness, not separate from anything, we rest in and as our deepest ground that is sometimes called our homeground or groundless ground.

As attention deepens and opens, our experience of and identification with the physical body changes. Our felt sense of the ground shifts accordingly. After decades of working with clients and students, I have observed a continuum of groundedness that spans four broad experiential stages: no ground, foreground, background, homeground. Each has a corresponding body identity. Charts are inadequate when trying to describe such subtle and fluid experience, but because the mind likes to detect patterns and share them, the following chart may help you to picture this continuum.

Stages of Groundedness	No ground	Foreground	Background	Homeground
Body Identity	"I am not in my body."	"I am in my body."	"My body is in me (as open awareness)."	"Everything is my body (as open awareness)."

No Ground

With the stage of no ground, it feels like we are barely in our bodies. We feel ungrounded. Our attention is on the surface or at a short distance from our body in a dissociative state. If we normally dwell in this stage as an adult, it is almost always because of childhood abuse or neglect. When we were being abused, it simply felt too dangerous to be present in the body. With neglect, it felt as if we weren't worth being attended to. Reworking this conditioning usually takes time. A safe, steady, and warmly attuned relationship allows attention to gradually reenter the body. Specialized somatic approaches also help.

We can experience temporary *states* of no ground when we are very ill or have been traumatized by an accident or an abrupt loss. Most of us have had tastes of this disembodied, ungrounded state. As an odd coincidence, as I was writing the previous sentence, my son came into my room to inform me that my car was missing. Sure enough, when I went outside, it was nowhere to be found. I briefly felt very ungrounded and disoriented. It turns out I had left the car parked at work two days before, and having immersed myself in writing at home, I had completely forgotten about it! Some people experience this ungrounded feeling through their whole lives.

Foreground

The foreground stage unfolds as we get more in touch with our needs and feelings. The interior of the body opens as we learn to feel our feelings and sense our sensations. Attention drops down from the head and into the trunk and core of the body. We can feel more of what is happening in the heart area and the gut. This is a big discovery for people who have been trained to overly rely on their thinking—something our information-saturated society increasingly cultivates. Most psychotherapy and somatic approaches focus on this domain, helping people to be more in touch with themselves on a personal level and more open to relating with others.

When we experience the foreground deeply, we feel very much in the body. As subtle dimensions awaken, essential qualities such as love, wisdom, inner strength, and joy emerge. The body begins to feel less dense and more like energy—porous and light.

Here is a description by John Greiner, one of my interviewees, that fits this stage of being richly foregrounded in his body:

> When I am in touch with the truth, there's a sense of calmness and being well-grounded. When I say calmness, it's throughout my whole body. It's a sense of being connected to the earth, almost as if there are roots. When I'm really grounded, it feels like it goes all the way to the center of the earth. It doesn't matter if I'm walking or I'm sitting, but that is a big part of my foundation.

Many spiritual approaches try to cultivate these subtle qualities and experiences so that they become stronger or last longer. While these practices can enhance the quality of personal life, they can also fuel an endless self-improvement project and delay the discovery of true inner freedom. Most psychospiritual approaches stop at this stage, satisfied with an enriched experience of the foreground.

Background

The background stage of awareness generally remains unrecognized, quietly out of view. It is like the page upon which words are written or the screen upon which a movie plays. It is the *context* within which the *contents* of awareness—thoughts, feelings, and sensations—arise. It is easily overlooked even though it is implicit in any experience. We cannot experience anything without awareness, yet when we try to objectify awareness, we can't. Looking for and trying to define it is like the eye trying to turn upon itself; what is seeing cannot be seen. As a result, the mind dismisses it.

Attention is like a wave on the ocean of awareness. Sometimes it peaks, focusing upon a particular experience, and other times it subsides back into its source. At some point, either because we have an intuition of this source or because we are seasick from the waves (suffering from our attachments and identifications), we become interested in following attention back toward its origin. This exploration may take the form of an intense, heartfelt inquiry—"What is this that is aware? Who am I really?"—or a simple, meditative resting in silence. It is more of an orientation than a technique.

As attention comes to rest quietly in the heart, not knowing, the background eventually comes into conscious awareness. At some point, we recognize that this is who we really are—infinite, open, empty, awake awareness. This recognition brings great freedom as we see that we are not bounded by space or time. We are not at all who we thought we were. No story or image can define or confine us. When we recognize our true nature as this unbounded awareness, we experience our body as being inside us, much like a cloud within the clear sky. Some spiritual traditions stop here, content with this transcendent realization.

When I was a professor at the California Institute of Integral Studies a few years ago, one of my students, Dan Scharlack, who had been a Buddhist meditator for years, approached me and asked if I would be there for him, as he was going through an intense spiritual opening. Without thinking I agreed, although we had only recently met and I did not know what "being there" would entail. It turned out that my offer of support was all that he needed. He came back a week or two later and reported having had the following dramatic experience:

> I just wanted to let go into the emptiness, no matter
> what happened. It was strange, but as soon as the
> decision arose, there was also spontaneously a sense
> that I actually knew how to move into and through it.
> Nevertheless I felt like I wanted someone there with
> me when I did it in case something bad happened. . . .
> As I came to the same impasse, I felt my torso
> begin to shake. My heart was beating so fast that it felt
> like it would come out of my chest. My whole body
> moved in violent convulsions that almost sent me off
> the [meditation] cushion. I jerked forward, then back,
> and everything inside of me felt like it was screaming.
> My body was convulsing as it never had before. In

spite of all of this, there was a sense that I just had to stay with the emptiness no matter what. There was a feeling of deep surrender, and I knew in that moment that I was willing to die for this.

And then it just kind of popped. I felt awareness move up my spine, out of the back of my heart, and out through the top of my head. While the shaking continued, it was less violent, and it was as if I was watching it from above and behind my body. Everything was incredibly quiet, and I had the unmistakable sense of looking down on my body from above with a deep feeling of compassion and sweetness for the one who was shaking.

When I finally opened my eyes, it was as if I was looking at the world for the first time. Everything felt crisp, alive, and fascinating.

Dan's experience illustrates a marked shift of attention and identity from the foreground to the background stage of awareness. It was an initial awakening to his true nature.

Homeground

A final stage of discovery awaits—the realization of our homeground. Even when we know ourselves as the background, a subtle duality continues between background and foreground, the knower and the known. The true nature of the body and, by extension, the world remains to be fully discovered. The felt sense of infinite awareness begins to saturate the body, often from the top down, as it penetrates into the core and transforms our emotional and instinctual levels of experience. It almost always takes years for this awareness to deeply unfold. As this happens, the body and the world feel increasingly transparent. We realize that the world is our body. The distinction between the background and the foreground, knower and known, dissolves. There is only knowing. Everything is seen and felt as an expression of awareness. There is a deep sense of being at home, as no-thing and everything. We could also speak of this as a groundless ground, a ground that is nowhere and everywhere. Words fail to capture it fully.

In 2010, I visited the Pech Merle cave in France, one of the few caves with extensive prehistoric paintings that remain open to the public. Since an earlier visit to Lascaux, I have been fascinated by these elegant charcoal and pigment drawings of horses, bison, aurochs (Paleolithic cattle), and mammoths, along with an occasional human handprint, some of which date as far back as 33,000 BCE. I have been equally drawn to the dark, silent caves that shelter these exquisite works of art.

Early one morning my wife, Christiane, and I joined a small group moving down a flight of stairs from a well-lit gift shop to the entrance of the cave about one hundred feet below. We stepped through the doorway into a completely different world—dark, cool, and unimaginably silent.

After a brief orientation, our guide warned us to stay together and began to lead us along a dimly lit path through the winding underground caverns. Despite her admonition, I felt compelled to hold back. As her voice and the footsteps of the others became increasingly faint in the darkness, I savored the extraordinary silence. The dark space beneath the earth and the feeling of open ground deep within my body became one ground—vibrant, dark, and mysterious. The outer and inner ground were not different; there was no separate knower and something known. I felt completely at home and at peace in the silence. There was a clear sense of knowing this homeground. Reluctantly, I rejoined the group after a few minutes.

Experiencing the Four Stages

Our sense of groundedness and our identification with our body are usually fairly stable and tend to localize in a particular stage somewhere along the continuum. For most people, it is localized in the foreground stage, where we experience being in our bodies. In contrast, our inner somatic, emotional, and mental states fluctuate according to many factors—health, stress, and occasional epiphanies—so that we can feel more or less grounded at any particular moment. States are constantly in flux, while stages change slowly. For instance, if I learn of the unexpected death of a close friend, I may experience a temporary state of being ungrounded, as if the rug has been pulled out from beneath me. The shock of the news may trigger me to feel dissociated for a while. In this case, my attention temporarily regresses from the stage of foreground to the stage of no ground. After a short time, my center of ground will return to its familiar stage.

If we usually feel fairly dissociated and ungrounded due to a chaotic childhood and then settle into a stable relationship as an adult, our stage of ground may gradually change from no ground to foreground. Instead of feeling mostly out of our body, we will feel mostly in our body. Effective psychotherapy can help facilitate this shift in stages.

As our spiritual life opens, we may begin to have experiences of being open and less identified with our body. At first these experiences may be fleeting glimpses or states. At some point, we may shift from the stage of feeling that we are in our body to the stage of sensing that we are open awareness within which our body exists. The sense of groundedness opens into a vast space. Everything that we have taken ourselves to be—sensations (body), feelings, and thoughts—is witnessed as an object in awareness. This is the background stage. As this open awareness penetrates deeply into the conditioned body, we begin to experience the world much more intimately. We have the sense that everything is made of this awareness and that nothing is separate from us. This fourth stage is our homeground.

These four stages—no ground, foreground, background, and homeground—don't always unfold in a smooth order. We can even skip a stage and revisit it later, although this is quite rare. For example, it is possible to be in a dissociative stage of no ground and suddenly be catapulted into the background stage of formless awareness. This uncommon event can leave someone feeling simultaneously spacy (dissociative) and spacious (open and unattached). I know a woman who experiences this. Her integrative work is to come more into her body—to better know the foreground. Doing so will also allow her to feel her homeground, her essential nonseparation from everything, including her body.

It is much more common for the gravity of identity to shift from foreground to background, from being someone to being no one, as

Dan experienced. This is a very significant opening; however, at some point, attention returns to the foreground of human feelings to accomplish a thorough, integrative "mopping up." Nothing is left behind in this process of embodying awareness. As Adyashanti poetically notes, "Love returns for itself."[4]

It is very common to have brief glimpses of a more mature stage and then settle back into a familiar one. Almost everyone has experienced expansive states of consciousness that were induced by witnessing beauty, making love, being in the presence of a genuine teacher, meditating, ecstatic dancing and drumming, psychoactive substances, or for no apparent reason at all. It is as if a camera lens temporarily opens and we are exposed to a much wider perspective. The doors of perception briefly clear.

Spiritual seekers often get attached to these experiences and try unsuccessfully to recreate them. These foretastes ignite a yearning to return home, along with confusion about how this return happens. While we cannot manufacture these openings, we can make ourselves available to them. A regular sitting meditation practice can be helpful, if it is done innocently. Likewise, self-inquiry helps to bring space from our beliefs and identities. When our attention opens to the felt sense of the ground, it is important to give ourselves fully to it. If it closes, then it is important to carefully observe the process. How do we unenlighten ourselves? What old stories and identities do we take on? Each glimpse of our deeper nature widens our capacity and reorients the body-mind.

It is also very common for attention to regress to a prior stage. In fact, this is an inevitable part of an integrative process that effectively explores and develops the foreground of individual feelings and needs. If we are willing to feel our feelings and sense our sensations, we will encounter unintegrated parts of the psyche. Temporary regression is inevitable and necessary. We go back through prior conditioning (in the present) to unpack, release, and reclaim what is of value. Inner child work is an example of this. The unfolding process is dynamic and unique for each of us. It is important to trust and follow it.

Even as reality is inherently grounding, it is also inherently ungrounding if we have not been living in accord with it. The truth is rarely convenient for those who have not been friends with it. For example, if I am used to being heavily armored in my body and out of touch with my feelings, it can be very disorienting when an interior sensitivity begins to open. I may feel vulnerable and shaky until I get used to the new sensations and the feelings of intimacy they bring. Similarly, if my work or relationships have been out of integrity, facing this reality can initially be very destabilizing.

On a deeper level, if I have strongly identified with being just this physical body and discover that who I am is the light of pure awareness empty of any definition, I may also feel very unsettled. Or I may be hugely relieved. Meditators will sometimes experience each of these polarities at different times, particularly on longer retreats. When this process goes through an especially intense phase, it can feel like we are both living in and *are* a house that is being remodeled.

Not surprisingly, the felt sense of the ground is often directly related to the root chakra at the base of the spine. When there is a strong contraction in this energy center, there is a weak felt sense of the ground. This chakra is one of the key strongholds of the inner grip. As I mentioned in chapter 2, this contraction directly relates to the fear of survival, either physically or psychologically. The threat of psychological annihilation usually appears as a fear of abandonment ("I'll be all alone"), engulfment ("I'll be smothered"), or fragmentation ("I'll fall apart and go crazy").

When we have lived with this contraction for many years, it becomes a shallow ground of its own—a kind of thin ice. It is as if we take our stand upon a familiar, although highly unstable, inner island of suffering. We become surprisingly attached to our chronic holding patterns; they give us a self-definition in the same way that living in a prison allows us to identify as a prisoner. Separating from them can be like prying a child away from her abusive parents. Clients will sometimes describe these contracted energetic and emotional states as "comfort zones," but they are anything but comfortable.

Letting go can feel like a freefall. I was once working with a client whose longtime friend had lost her son to suicide. My client had known the young man his whole life, and it was a devastating loss for everyone. As she closed her eyes and let her attention drop down and in, she sensed a contraction at the base of her spine. As she felt into it, it suddenly released, and she had the image of a trapdoor opening and her body free falling into dark, empty space. Instead of panicking, however, she relaxed into the feeling of being held by no-thing and experienced a clear sense of nonseparation from everything. In that moment, the ground was wide open—or perhaps I should say that she was wide open to her homeground.

Eckhart Tolle experienced this shift into the background stage at age twenty-nine, when he was a very depressed graduate student at the University of Cambridge. One night he awoke with a feeling of complete dread, loathing the world and longing for annihilation. He had the repetitive thought that he could no longer live with himself:

> Then suddenly I became aware of what a peculiar thought it was. "Am I one or two? If I cannot live with myself, there must be two of me: the 'I' and the 'self' that 'I' cannot live with." Maybe, I thought, only one of them is real.
>
> I was so stunned by this strange realization that my mind stopped. I was fully conscious, but there were no more thoughts. Then I felt drawn into what seemed like a vortex of energy. It was a slow movement at first and then accelerated. I was gripped by an intense fear, and my body started to shake. I heard the words "resist nothing" as if spoken inside my chest. I could feel myself being sucked into a void. It felt as if the void was inside myself rather than outside. Suddenly there was no more fear, and I let myself fall into that void. I have no recollection of what happened after that.[5]

There are a number of interesting elements in Tolle's experience. First, he was desperately depressed; life held no interest for him. Second, his mind was stopped by a paradoxical thought—a naturalistic koan: was he one or two selves? If he was two, perhaps one of them was not real. Third, his familiar identity began to collapse and along with it the sense of ground as he felt sucked down an energetic vortex and into a void within himself. And, finally, although he was terrified, he trusted an inner voice inside his chest that counseled him to not resist. He completely let go into a free fall. He was like the mountaineer in the earlier parable, except that he was able to trust his inner knowing. When Tolle woke up in the morning, he reported, he felt as if he had been born into a fresh and pristine world.

Our sense of groundedness has different flavors as other essential qualities emerge with it. For example, there may be feelings of love, flow, and a connection with being. When I interviewed my friend Riyaz Motan, a psychotherapist, he described his evolving sense of the ground in this way:

> Just as we talked about [the ground], I sensed it immediately as a rootedness—of energy going down through the feet and out into the earth. Even the earth doesn't quite describe it—just a sense of rootedness into ground. The image of a pyramid comes, that feels really wide with a solid base.
>
> As I sense the ground more, part of what happens is the heart comes more into it. There is a sense of receptivity, empathy, and softness. There is a dual quality of real solidity and strength and yet softness, receptivity, and openness.

Being in touch with the felt sense of the ground as a solid, rooted base allows the heart to open. The safer we feel, the more easily we can sustain an open heart.

When I spoke with Silke Greiner, a gifted bodyworker, she described a deeper level of groundedness that arose when she connected with being:

> JP: As you described that connection [with being] coming into awareness, you moved your hands upward from the ground.
>
> Silke: Right.

JP: The sense of connection becomes clearer and more alive for you.

Silke: Yeah, I guess it's very deep. When it's just a relative truth, it is not as deep. This really is what I'm describing when I'm down into the truth of being because I'm not always as aware of it in my day-to-day life. But when I'm really sitting down, when I'm working [bodywork/massage], I take that space and open myself to it. The truth of being just appears.

Silke contrasted her experience of being relatively grounded in everyday life with a deeper sense of groundedness and connection that she opened to when she sat and worked with people. The "truth of being" came clearly into her awareness. This sense is available to each of us at any moment if we are willing to slow down and listen. Doing so is like turning our face toward an invisible sun. We just need to remember that it is here awaiting our attention.

Summary

As we attune with inner knowing, we experience a deep relaxation in the core of our body and a growing sense of groundedness. However, most of us are in a state of chronic inner tension as we try to subtly (and sometimes not so subtly) control ourselves and the environment. Some of this tension is concerned with biological survival, while most of it is concerned with psychological survival—the preservation of the self-image. The psychological self—the little me—is always insecure and defends itself against potential annihilation. This manifests in the body as an attempt to hold ourselves up and in with an inner grip or core contraction. We can be forced to release this grip when we encounter a crisis that makes us let go of the illusion of control and/or brings the insight that it is futile and more painful to try to hang on. The chronic grip also softens as we live more authentically, both personally and essentially. Feeling held by something greater than our limited self also allows the letting go to happen more gracefully. Letting go requires trusting in life—no matter what.

Reality is inherently grounding. The more in touch with it we are, the more grounded we feel. This is true on every level: physical, mental, emotional, energetic, and spiritual. Reality can be temporarily ungrounding to us when we have been living out of accord with it.

There is a continuum of groundedness with distinctive stages that sometimes coexist: no ground, foreground, background, and homeground. Each stage has a corresponding body identification. Attention can move fluidly between stages, and we can experience foretastes, regressions, and an occasional gravitational shift of identity between stages.

The openness of the energy center at the base of the spine is directly related to the depth of experiencing groundedness. Letting go can sometimes feel like a free fall. Our felt sense of the ground deepens with our attunement with being and is often accompanied by the experience of other essential qualities such as love, connection, and flow.

Attuning with Relaxed Groundedness

Physically	Mentally	Emotionally	Energetically	Spiritually
Exercise regularly, daily if possible. Take at least a half hour walk. Eat a healthy, balanced diet and minimize snacking, sweets, and stimulants. Spend time in nature. Get enough sleep.	Recognize and question your limiting stories, especially those around survival.	Feel your feelings, especially fear. Be willing to speak and hear the truth with others, without projection or blame.	Bring your attention down into the lower belly. Breathe as if you are drawing your breath up from the earth and releasing it back down. Sense yourself being held by the ground. Practice qigong, tai chi, yoga, body sensing, and similar practices.	Open to the background awareness. Rest in and as it.

6

inner alignment

The truth always brings everything into alignment.
ADYASHANTI

Soo Jung began our session talking about something she rarely did—dancing at a costume party. She was concerned that she had appeared foolish and realized that she wanted to be seen as "decent." This was important to her because it compensated for an underlying feeling that she was "indecent, stained, and tainted." After some reflection, she wondered whether this desire to be seen as decent came from having been raped as a teen. She was afraid that this stain was visible to others and wanted to rid herself of it. I suggested that she could get in touch with that which was unstained, whole, and pure within herself.

"How do I find that road to purity?" she asked, as her hands pointed to the middle of her chest. When I reflected back where she was pointing, she was a bit startled to realize her body was already showing her where to go.

Sensing into her heart center, she said, "It feels like there are layers and layers of thorny bushes to cross."

"What is behind the thorns?" I asked.

"It seems far, but it's not. I don't know. Earlier it wasn't far. I can see the light," she said.

I suggested that her purity was very close and encouraged her to open to and intimately sense it. In a slow, soft voice she began to ask herself, "Where is my purity?"

There was a long silence.

Then I could feel something lighting up vertically in the core of my body. I told her that she was getting a response and asked her if she could sense it.

"It seems like it is here somewhere," she answered, arranging her hands one on top of the other along the centerline of her body, making a vertical motion.

"You are very clear and aligned. Stay with this attunement," I said.

To my surprise, she responded, "I can't stay here. I am going to combust!"

Soo Jung took a deep breath and made a loud "ahhhh" sound and began to shake. I encouraged her to relax into and trust her experience. She started to clap her hands more and more rapidly while making "ohhhh" sounds and taking deep breaths. Then she began to make vigorous outward movements from her chest with both hands and started to laugh.

"It wants to open," she said slowly and then added in a small child's voice, "The hole is very small."

"It is safe to come out now," I said.

"It's *not* okay. Someone will take it. I need to protect myself," she responded, continuing to rapidly clap her hands. Her shaking increased. She took some deep breaths, gradually calmed, and then started to sing and laugh.

She suddenly got up and walked rapidly around the office, exclaiming, "I want to, I want to, I want to come out! I want to go straight!"

She began to pose questions to herself and listen and feel for a response—a spontaneous form of self-inquiry.

"Where is my purity?" she again asked. She paused. "Yeah, inside, where inside?" Again she paused. "Everywhere! I want the specific location!" Another pause. "I don't know."

She then traced a vertical line in the air. "It goes all the way past my body to the ground." She also pointed upward. "It's a line."

"I am hot in the center," she added, gesturing to her solar plexus.

"What does it mean that I am pure?" she then asked. She playfully swung her arms like a little girl and began to dance. "I don't have to hide. I want to twirl." She laughed. "I feel so like a child, a baby. This is it. Purity was there as a baby!"

"The mind says, 'You are goofy, silly.' I don't want to be like this." She illustrated what she meant by tracing a square box in the air with her hands.

"I can do this!" she exclaimed as she continued to walk freely, moving her arms, laughing, and singing "la la la" like a delighted child.

Soo Jung's remarkable session beautifully illustrates the process of suddenly coming into alignment and the powerful sense of aliveness that this can unleash. When we allow space for our deepest truth to unfold, we never know what may pop out! In this case, it was an innocent, lively, and delighted little girl.

Soo Jung's concern about appearing "decent" led us to uncover her core limiting self-image and belief. She was convinced that something was wrong with her—she was "stained"—and that something, her purity, was lacking. She felt deeply ashamed and lived in constant fear of being exposed. She was desperate to conceal and somehow rid herself of this stain.

Regardless of the abuse or neglect we have experienced, the core of our being—open awareness—remains untouched and whole. I have witnessed my clients repeatedly discover that, while aspects of their psyche can be deeply wounded, our reality as pure awareness can never be hurt or diminished. These dimensions coexist, even as our psychological wounds may temporarily obscure the recognition of an underlying radiance. Knowing this, I pointed Soo Jung toward her inherent purity.

When she asked how to find this purity, her hands immediately responded by pointing toward her heart center. Our inner knowing uses a special sign language that often relates to one of the major energy centers (see chapter 2). Over the years I have learned to carefully watch my clients' hand movements as they speak. These gestures invariably portray what is closed and what wants to open on energetic and emotional levels.

The barrier of thorns symbolized Soo Jung's defense against opening her heart. It seemed impassable to her at first. Yet when she felt
into what was being protected—the purity behind the defense—she
sensed an inner vertical line that her hands automatically and elegantly
traced in front of her body. This gesture corresponded directly with
what I was sensing in the interior of my body—an emergent vertical
current of energy and light. I knew that we were both attuning and
aligning with something greater than either of us as individuals.

Soo Jung experienced a powerful inner fire. Tapping into this
intense frequency of energy caused her whole body to tremble. She
was both astonished and frightened by this sudden influx. Her sounds
and rapid clapping were her body's spontaneous attempts to both
contain and release it. Something deep inside was trying to open up.
When she burst out laughing, her hands portrayed an energy pouring
out from her heart center.

Although she was afraid that something essential would be taken
from her if she opened up, she also felt a deep desire to "come out" and
"go straight." These words reflected an emerging felt sense of the vertical
line that ran through the length of her body—deep into the earth and
high above. Once she had a clear sense of where her purity was, she
wanted to know what it *meant* to be pure. A joyful, dancing, and singing little girl leaped out in response. I felt deeply touched to witness
this spontaneous unfolding of innocence. Soo Jung was discovering that,
despite her abuse, her inner purity was intact. There was no essential
stain or lack. The same is true for all of us.

Verticality and the Current of Life

When we get in touch with our truth, we feel more inwardly aligned,
vertically upright, in our integrity, and alive. There is a subtle yet clear
sense of things falling into place and lining up inside. These qualities
relate to what I call the *current of life*. This powerful current is like a
great underground river that flows vertically through the core of the
body. It is a life energy that runs through each of us and yet is greater
than any of us. The more we are in our truth, the easier it is to sense.

Even if we don't sense it directly, we can recognize it indirectly as a sense of inner harmony and vibrancy.

Soo Jung was almost overwhelmed by her first direct contact with it. She feared that she would burst into flames. The separate sense of self, the little me that we mistake as our self, fears its demise when faced with this degree of radiance. Witnessing Soo Jung's initial encounter with the purity of being was like watching a novice whitewater rafter put into a river with class four rapids (very difficult). Soo Jung's self-trust and determination to come into deeper alignment with herself, combined with her sense of feeling held and encouraged by me, allowed her to take the plunge and navigate the tumultuous energies that she first encountered.

The first direct contact with pure being is often the most dramatic because of the contrast between our chronic state of contraction and the feeling of being opened wide. When this door first cracks open, it can feel like a pressure chamber releasing—there can be a big "whoosh." If we don't resist this opening, the body-mind will adjust over time, and a new balance will emerge.

Usually the sense of inner alignment shows up much less dramatically. Often my clients sit up straighter as they get in touch with their truth. I do the same when I am with them. It is a very curious phenomenon: the truth sits us up! Our bodies become more relaxed, grounded, *and* upright as we attune with the truth. When I asked my friend Debira Branscombe, a psychotherapist, about what it was like for her when her clients got in touch with their truth, she reported, "There is something very vertical. When I hear something true, there's an alignment that I experience that almost fixes my posture. It feels like this vertical alignment is another way of experiencing connection with each other and with life."

My clients and students also report that they can sense when they are listening to someone who is honestly expressing themselves. We can *feel* authenticity in ourselves and others. Something lines up, lights up, and rings true when this happens. We are more engaged, alert, and upright. This felt sense guides my work with people who are exploring the truth of their experience. My body lets me know when they are on or off the mark, when they are honing in or wandering away from the truth. Many of my clients are able to do the same as they learn to listen to their bodies. Their attention fine-tunes the instrument of their sensitivity.

EXPERIMENT *Sensing Inner Alignment*

Reflect on a recent time when you felt that you were in your truth, either personally or essentially. What is your bodily sense as you attune with this now? Notice what happens to your posture as you do so.

Also recall a time when you were with someone whom you experienced as being deeply authentic. What did you sense in your body as you listened?

Pay attention to your bodily sense of truth when you are with people during the next few days. ●

Arthur Giacalone, a clinical psychologist, described to me his experience of aligning with the truth this way: "There is a . . . sense of living and being aligned in and through the vertical axis of the body, with the gestalt of my physicality being perfectly proportioned around this experience—an energetic rightness and clarity that ascends from a basic feeling of earthly groundedness."

For Arthur, the sense of alignment rises from the ground. This corresponds with an ascending life current. In his case, this alignment is accompanied by other essential qualities: lightness and clarity.

Silke Greiner, the bodyworker whom you met in the previous chapter, also reported a strong connection between being grounded and feeling a sense of verticality:

> There's a vertical line. For me it is somehow the connection between heaven and earth that goes through me—a very powerful way to be in the world. If I am going off that line, I am not in my truth. When I am connected to the line, I am in my truth. That's why the line is so important for me.

If I am not grounded in it, it wouldn't work if I just go up, and it wouldn't work if I just go down. So it's that whole flow of energy that connects that.

Silke feels that she is in her truth when she is "on line" in a vertical flow of energy that includes overhead and underground dimensions—heaven and earth. As humans, our experience of life ranges from the earthly and practical dimension of physical survival to subtle levels of perception to infinite awareness. Our sense of the truth includes all of these levels, from the densest form to spacelike formlessness.

EXPERIMENT *Feeling Your Verticality*

Find a comfortable, quiet place to sit upright, close your eyes, and relax. Take a few breaths and let your attention settle down and in.

Imagine that your body is suspended by a thin yet very strong thread at the very top of your head. This gives a sense of the vertical line that runs from the top of your head all the way down through your body and deep into the ground.

Follow that line down through the core of the earth and beyond. Let your attention rest here for a minute.

Then track it back upward through your body high into space. Feel your full vertical extension. Is there an endpoint in either direction?

Rest in and as this verticality. ◉

Many years ago I attended a public talk where Jean Klein invited us to "remember your verticality." This phrase struck me deeply because it was one of the first times that I could clearly sense this verticality. Jean associated this sense of verticality with being. When we are in touch with it, we feel ourselves in timeless presence, unbounded by space or time. Jean referred to the process of evolution, personal and collective, as *becoming* and associated it with the horizontal dimension. As humans, we live in both dimensions, the horizontal and the vertical—in and out of time. Time unfolds within the timeless. These two essential dimensions of human life find their meeting place in the heart.

There are ascending and descending currents within this verticality. The ascending current is associated with *waking up* out of our limited identifications. It is a movement of *transcendence,* a going beyond all form. This is usually the initial movement of awakening in which we deeply realize that we are none of the things (thoughts, feelings, and sensations) that we thought we were. The descending current is associated with a *waking down.* It is a movement of *immanence* where open awareness moves more deeply into form, saturating the emotional and instinctual levels of the body. A balanced approach to spirituality honors both dimensions and recognizes that the divine is found in form as much as in the formless. To use theological language, these are the two faces of God. When we live in a balanced way, honoring the transcendent and the immanent, we can sense a seamlessness to life.

When I spoke with Riyaz Motan, whom you also met in the last chapter, he described experiencing a sense of this seamless alignment, ascending and descending currents, and a feeling that there was nobody and no body when he was most deeply in touch with the truth:

> Riyaz: The experience in the body is just feeling in complete alignment. There is a seamlessness. I could almost say that there is nobody because it just feels like energy, continuity, and connection. . . . I get images of currents moving through the body.

> JP: Do the currents move in any particular direction?

> Riyaz: When I am really feeling connected with more of a spiritual truth, a sense of wholeness, there is a current moving through the body vertically. . . . Maybe it starts that way and then becomes multidirectional. It feels both up and down.

JP: Ascending and descending?

Riyaz: Ascending and descending—a sense of a
subtle current in the sense of alignment. The body
feels less solid and more energetic, subtle and fluid.

JP: And you were saying that it is almost as if there
is no body?

Riyaz: Yes. In the deepest experiences there's
really a lack of a sense of self and with that there's
a lack of the sense of body. And yet, interestingly
enough, if I tune in to it, there is a body, a sense
of body but it is a . . . more subtle experience of
the body.

JP: How is this different from a state of dissociation?

Riyaz: (Pause.) It is completely the opposite of
dissociation. It feels connected. I am so connected
that the seams aren't experienced. That's what
it feels like. Dissociation feels like complete
disconnection. There is no sense of the body
because I am disconnected from my body. Whereas
this is a sense of feeling so completely in the body
that the body is completely in me in the sense that
there's a seamless quality.

This last point reflects how paradoxical language becomes when we try
to express a subtle experience: we can feel so completely in the body
that the body feels as if it is in us. This marks the shift of attention from
the foreground to the background that I mentioned in chapter 5. It is
also important to recognize the difference between the deeply grounded
state of seamless alignment and "being nobody" that Riyaz describes
and a dissociative state of no ground.

Integrity

When we are inwardly aligned, we are in our integrity. *Integrity* means "a state of honesty and wholeness." (Some definitions include "moral uprightness"—there's the vertical dimension again.) Honesty is a key element of alignment. When we are dishonest with ourselves and others, we are out of alignment and out of integrity. Being honest with ourselves means to face the facts of our experience—to be willing to feel what we are feeling, sense what we are sensing, and question all of our cherished beliefs. It also means that there is congruence between what we think, feel, say, and do. If our life is not congruent with our deeper knowing, we can sense it. We feel off inside. Coming into integrity is a dynamic, ongoing process.

Being honest with others means to tell the unarguable truth. This means that we stop blaming others for our experience. No one makes us feel as we do. How we feel is our responsibility. We may get triggered by others' words or actions, but it is still up to us to examine our reactivity. Telling the truth does not mean dumping our judgments or reactions onto others, although it is often framed this way. A true honesty leads us to look at our part in a situation and acknowledge it. It also leads us to question who we really are. So many of our reactions arise because we hear (or imagine we hear) someone else saying what we secretly believe about ourselves—that something is terribly flawed or lacking in our core. This was Soo Jung's fear—she thought she was stained. We think we are these images and beliefs with which we identify.

Honesty also requires an equal willingness to hear the truth of others. We are generally eager to speak but slow to listen. To listen does not necessarily mean that we agree. We stay open to the possibility that there is something that we don't understand or didn't know, open to our own blind spots and misinterpretations, open to learning, yet knowing we don't need to accept another person's version of reality if it does not truly resonate with us. There is always a chance of us misunderstanding another person's truth. As I get older, I am able to acknowledge how frequently I misunderstand others. It is a humbling process! Yet it is also refreshing to admit the truth of my limitations.

It is beautiful and very encouraging to know that our bodies are sensitive to the truth and offer us subtle feedback when we are in or out of accord with it. When I interviewed Adyashanti at his home in 2007 about the bodily experience of truth, he spoke in terms of an inner alignment and resonance:

> JP: In addition to the feeling of relief [when we are in touch with the truth], there's also a sense of rightness that is lively, clear, and radiant.

> Adya: That's what I think of as that moment of resonance, where everything lines up inside. There is that feeling of that light. To me, the truth always brings everything into alignment. . . . One of my favorite definitions comes from Zen where it says [that enlightenment is] the harmonization of body and mind. It is the feeling where everything clicks. On an energetic level, everything clicks, so there is no disharmony.

> JP: It is a sense of alignment.

> Adya: That alignment gives the sense of an inner tuning fork in perfect pitch. That's that inner feeling. . . . To me that's what any kind of expression or teaching of truth is really aimed at—that inner alignment and inner resonance. If it brings that, wonderful. If it doesn't bring that, then it hasn't really served its purpose in that moment.

For Adya, *alignment, attunement, resonance,* and *inner harmony* are different ways to describe the most important impact of a spiritual teaching. Each of us has an "inner tuning fork" that can sense when this is happening and, equally importantly, when it is not. All authentic spiritual teaching is about facilitating this inner knowing.

Here is Adya again, from the same interview:

> My sense is that we are biologically hooked up for the
> truth in the sense that as soon as we go into any illusion
> at all, the body has discord. Immediately it is sensed
> in the body. And to me that's the way that the body
> is constantly telling us if we are in accord or out of
> accord with just the way things really are. For me, I see
> it as either sensing the truth of something, which has
> a certain feeling, or sensing the untruth, which is even
> easier because it is just some level of discord.

Indeed, it is easier to sense when we are out of accord with the truth.
There is a feeling of inner discord. When I am out of accord or I sense
it in others, I feel ungrounded and/or queasy in the gut or the heart
areas. It is important to recognize how this felt sense of discord shows
up for each of us.

EXPERIMENT *Sensing Being Out of Integrity*

Take a minute to remember a time when you were not acting
in your integrity—when you went against your inner knowing.
What is your bodily felt sense of this?

Aliveness Versus Excitement

The sense of inner alignment is intimately related to aliveness. It is
hard to speak of one without the other. When we are more aligned
with the truth, we also feel more alive. We light up inside and feel ourselves in a greater flow. When this happens with my clients, students,
friends, and colleagues, they report a feeling of inner vibrancy and talk
about a greater sense of aliveness. Why is this?

I suspect it is because we are tapping into a much deeper life energy,
something that is unconcerned with the self-image—the little me.
The less self-concern we have, the more freely this underground life

current begins to move in our daily lives. Our primary approach to life shifts from wondering, "What's in it for me?" or "What can I get or avoid?" to "What is life asking of me?" Our attention and intention move out of the little eddy of the ego into a great river, from the part to the whole. Greater energy, power, and responsibility come with this movement. Gandhi used the Sanskrit term *satyagraha*—"truth force"—to describe this power. He knew it firsthand. So did Nelson Mandela and Martin Luther King Jr. Environmental activists and educators who are focused on the health of the planet, such as Al Gore and Bill McKibben, who founded 350.org, are also tapped into this. However, we don't need to be an actor on the world stage to express this. Every spontaneous act of kindness and honesty comes from this source of life that is so much greater than the ego.

It is important to distinguish the sense of aliveness from the experience of excitement. The sense of aliveness arises from the core of our being. We feel it somewhere deep inside ourselves. While powerful, it is generally quiet. Aliveness stands on its own; it is autonomous yet deeply connected with the whole. We can feel it regardless of circumstances—whether we are alone or with others, quiet or active, sick or healthy. While this aliveness is responsive, creative, and engaged, it is also unattached to outcomes. Aliveness doesn't grab or push away; it doesn't need to. It is an expression of fullness.

We feel excited when our minds, emotions, or bodies are stimulated. Excitement is a completely natural and healthy phenomenon. As humans we need stimulation; we thrive when we are "touched" on various levels, whether we are running through sprinklers or being hugged as a child, listening to music or dancing as an adult, meeting a dear friend for lunch, engaged in a deep conversation, doing meaningful work, or watching our favorite sports team or TV program.

On the other hand, we can be easily excited by delusion. Fundamentalists, religious or political, become very excited when someone agrees or disagrees with them. And, if we are honest with ourselves, we can see that we are all fundamentalists when it comes to our own stories about reality. Just notice how you react when you listen to someone who has a different point of view.

Some people are very attached to emotional drama as a way to feel alive. They may display intense emotions such as rage or despair, yet there is a curious lack of authentic feeling. When I watch someone going through this, I feel as if I am witnessing, to borrow from Shakespeare, a tale of sound and fury signifying nothing. There is lots of excitement, but no real life. The core is numb, and the histrionics are a smokescreen. When people are easily enraged, I am always more interested in their underlying hurt and vulnerability. On the other hand, people who suppress their anger and rage may need to get in touch with it. A life-protecting and -affirming power is buried deep within rage, even if this power is expressed in a distorted form.

When we feel cut off from an underlying sense of aliveness, we usually try to numb ourselves through some form of self-medication, or alternatively, we try to stimulate ourselves. It seems that modern society is increasingly oriented toward hyperstimulation, particularly through electronic media, as people feel increasingly disconnected and bored. Commercials famously try to generate it. Recently, my son showed me a video ad of a young man bonding with his new car. When the man touched the car, the pupils of his eyes flared in soulful contact, just as in the film *Avatar* when the native people's eyes widened as they bonded with their flying creatures, the mountain banshees. The ad appealed to an intuitive longing for release from separation and a deeper connection to something greater. It was both clever and sad.

We try to know an essential aliveness by acquiring objects and having experiences, but it never works—not for long. As Jean Klein noted, "The object never fulfills its promise." That said, I am very fond of my little sports car—a pale version of a mountain banshee! We can deeply enjoy what life offers, especially as we know that it will soon pass. Excitement, in the sense that I am referring to it, is not a marker of inner knowing by itself. We are too easily seduced and excited by our stories, hopes, desires, and fears. We can feel excited without feeling alive and alive without feeling excited. When those feelings coincide, it's lovely.

EXPERIMENT *Distinguishing Aliveness from Excitement*

Think of a time when you felt most alive. What is the inner feeling? Are you able to distinguish this from excitement? What is the difference? ●

Summary

The sense of inner alignment is one of the primary markers of being in touch with our inner knowing. There is a sense of things lining up and falling into place inside. An inner verticality opens up that we can sense as a line running through the core of the body, extending high above and far beneath. One manifestation of this verticality is that we sit up straighter when we are being authentic or when we sense authenticity in others. This verticality is connected to a current of life that flows through the core of our body and all living beings. As we become more inwardly aligned and less self-centered, we become more open to this current and more in service to the whole of life.

Inner alignment corresponds with inner integrity. Honesty with ourselves and others supports this integrity. Honesty with ourselves means facing our experience just as it is and being intimate with it—feeling our feelings, sensing our sensations, and questioning our beliefs. Doing so brings greater congruence between our thoughts, feelings, words, and actions. Honesty also means being willing to tell the unarguable truth and hear it from others.

Inner alignment also brings a sense of aliveness, which differs from excitement. Aliveness is autonomous, free of any circumstances. Excitement requires stimulation of the body, mind, and feelings. While it is natural and healthy to be excited, we can be stimulated by our erroneous beliefs. Aliveness and excitement sometimes coincide.

Attuning with Inner Alignment

Physically	Mentally	Emotionally	Energetically	Spiritually
Acquaint yourself with the sense of sitting or standing relaxed and upright.

Notice how you feel in the heart and gut areas when you are in or out of accord with your inner knowing. | Commit to being honest in your self-observation.

Question those rationalizations and excuses that undermine your integrity and sense of inner alignment. | Tell the unarguable truth of your experience without blaming yourself or others.

Be equally willing to hear it. | Sense the vertical line that extends through the core of your body in both directions without an endpoint.

Notice the subtle ascending and descending life currents that run through your body and how they may correspond with your thoughts, feelings, actions, and inner knowing. | Make a commitment to yourself to live in accord with your deepest truth. Then work steadily and compassionately toward keeping it. |

7

openheartedness

The Heart is another name for Reality
and this is neither inside nor outside the body.

RAMANA MAHARSHI

I have been mentoring Kelly for the past few years. She is a member of one of my self-inquiry groups, and from time to time we meet individually for a period of quiet gazing and conversation. There is an immediate resonance when we sit together. She tends to quickly drop into her body and courageously explore her arising experience. I asked her to write about one of our recent sittings, since it beautifully illustrates the theme of this chapter. Here is her account:

> As we sat together, I became aware of a strong sensation in the heart, almost like a physical pressure. John invited me to be with it, and I realized it was a fear of death. When John remarked, "Yes, something does die," I had an immediate intuition of a willingness to let go. The fear wasn't a problem. In the next moments, there was a sense of the totality taking over, and my heart felt a knowing and a resting in that. It felt clear to keep surrendering to the feeling of the totality taking over. There was a sense

of spaciousness, nonseparateness, light, and a sense of
my whole being, no longer localized but bright and shiny.
As the session neared the end, I felt a trust, both in the
process of meeting myself in this way and also in the
continual surrender that was being asked of me.

I could sense a contraction at the back of Kelly's heart as I sat with
her. There was a strong movement toward opening and releasing, yet
there was also a subtle resistance. Once she was able to name it as the
fear of death, a letting go spontaneously happened. She surrendered to
the totality, to wholeness. For the separate sense of self, this surrender
looks and feels like a kind of death, yet it is a profound opening into
space and light. The heart center (see chapter 2) is one of the primary
portals for this discovery.

Openheartedness is one of the most easily recognizable somatic
markers of inner knowing. The heart is a highly sensitive center of
feeling and knowing. It has many levels and remarkable depth. It is
our most intimate area, the one we are quickest to protect. We often
touch ourselves in the heart area when we are referring to ourselves
or when we are feeling close to another. When the heart area is open,
there is a subtle sense of warmth, expansion, sweetness, and aliveness.
We feel loving and connected. A different quality of knowing emerges,
one that is spontaneous, direct, and unconcerned with outcomes. Our
willingness to not know, to not rely on our ordinary thinking mind for
guidance, and to let attention rest in the heart area opens up a door
to a different way of knowing. As we do so, we become much more
accepting and compassionate with ourselves and others.

If our heart has been closed and then begins to open, we often discover why our native sensitivity originally shut down. Old emotional
wounds will surface and ask for our attention. Difficult feelings such
as grief, shame, self-loathing, personal deficiency, despair, and fear can
arise. We may feel sensations and see images of embedded shards or
an apparently bottomless dark pit. Most of these emotionally painful
layers are personal and relational in origin, the results of old betrayals,
disappointments, abandonments, and assaults. Some are existential,

shared by all humans, such as Kelly's fear of dying and being no one. Opening our hearts requires courage, dedication, and a willingness to be deeply vulnerable. As this opening happens, it is important that we meet our old wounds and contractions with understanding and compassion.

A great deal of my work with people is helping them to get out of their heads and into their hearts. As I mentioned in chapter 2, the spiritual journey is in large part about this transition. When our attention naturally rests in the heart center, we feel at home in ourselves and the world. We have easy access to the wisdom of the heart.

Following the Path of the Heart

We are often encouraged to "follow our hearts," but what does this really mean? How can we tell if we are ensnared in some delusion and riding an emotional fantasy or listening to true inner guidance? The inner knowing of the heart is often obscured by fears, desires, and limiting beliefs. How do we go forward with any confidence? It seems that we must *feel* our way forward, step by step, continually listening and adjusting as we go.

Following the path of the heart requires discernment. Love needs to be tempered by wisdom. Heart wisdom is a combination of love and clear understanding. Love without wisdom is naïve and easily leads to disastrous relationships, as almost all of us can attest to. Love can blind us so that we see only what we want to in the other person. The honeymoon phase of a relationship reflects this strong tendency to idealize. We hope so much that the other will fulfill us that we happily overlook their needs and limitations. Discernment—clear-sightedness—pierces these illusions without devaluing the other. It allows us to have a balanced view and to see them as they are.

If we follow our heart wisdom and things don't work out as we expect, it doesn't necessarily mean that we have made a misstep. There may be a vital lesson that we needed to learn. In fact, there is no objective way to determine if we have done the "right" thing. Our lives unfold more like meandering rivers than freeways. One thing is clear: if we are generating more suffering for ourselves and others, it is important to slow down and take an honest and intimate look at how we are functioning.

When I talk about trustworthy guidance with my clients and students, I emphasize that our *inner* guidance is ultimately what we need to rely on. The rest of our guidance comes from the law, societal norms, and family conditioning. These external guides have their legitimate roles to play; however, in the end we must check inside to feel what is true for ourselves. At some point we have to kick off the training wheels and trust our inner sense of balance. I have trusted this inner guidance with all of my major decisions around career, relationships, and spiritual path. I am grateful that I have, even as this process has led to some highly unlikely twists and turns. I never would have guessed that my life would unfold as it has.

There were some critical junctures in my life where the wisdom of the heart revealed itself, and I decided to act on it. Sometimes it came as a quiet knowing in the heart, other times in a vision or dream. Reflecting back on my life, I can see that I usually needed to admit my confusion and ask for guidance before I was in touch with it. Humility was important. I offer the following example from my first marriage to encourage you to trust your inner knowing and follow it.

I briefly met Linda at an Association for Transpersonal Psychology conference in Pacific Grove, California, in 1981. We both signed up for a weekend workshop on developing intuition, which would take place the following month in San Francisco. Although Linda came to the workshop with her boyfriend, she and I paired up in a dyad and mutually experienced a profound connection. I felt like we had known each other in another life—some ancient recognition had reawakened. It seemed that she knew my heart from the inside. At the end of the workshop, she told me that her teacher, the venerable Tibetan Buddhist master Kalu Rinpoche, would be giving a talk the following night. Did I want to come? Of course!

I arrived at the door of the hall at exactly the same time as Linda, who had her boyfriend in tow. We sat next to each other, and during Kalu's talk, I felt my energy body completely blend with hers. To my astonishment, it felt as if an inner marriage had occurred, yet there was nothing I could say about it. So instead, I said a friendly good-bye. I broke off my relationship with my girlfriend the next day and asked Linda out on a date that weekend. It turned out that she had experienced the same thing sitting next to me at Kalu's talk. On our second date two days later, I proposed to her, and she accepted. As I drove home, I was stunned at what I had done. It was completely out of character with my normally cautious style. And Linda still needed to tell her boyfriend!

When we met again a few days later, Linda revealed that she had a number of life-threatening illnesses, including pulmonary hypertension, and offered to release me from my commitment. I was again stunned and inwardly torn. The inner connection felt so true, yet the outer circumstances looked impossible. Linda had a life expectancy of five years, according to her doctors, and no savings or health insurance. I was a grad student with little money. How could this relationship possibly work? My mind told me that it was completely insane to marry her, while my heart told me to stay. After agonizing for several days, I decided to follow my heart and go ahead with the engagement.

Linda was hospitalized several months before our marriage and needed a medical team to pull her back from the edge of death. She lived for nearly seven more years, and we enjoyed a wonderful relationship. At the time, I had never felt so intimately known and loved in my life. Although the last years were very difficult for both of us as her health declined, I never regretted my decision to marry her.

At the beginning of January 1989, Linda told me that she would die in twenty-eight days. She asked me if I knew who would be my next partner. It was a sincere question, and I knew it deserved an honest response. I told her that I thought it would be Christiane, whom we both knew through the Jean Klein fellowship. There was no outer reason for me to think this since Christiane and I were just friends at the time. Linda nodded and said Christiane would be a good partner for me. Twenty-eight days later, Linda went into a diabetic coma and was taken to the hospital by paramedics. She was discharged and returned home briefly before again losing consciousness in the early hours the next morning.

She was rushed to the hospital, but this time she did not recover. Her death was only a few hours later than she had predicted.

When I saw her lifeless body full of tubes at 2 a.m. in the vacant emergency room, I knew that it was not Linda. It was her body, and she was clearly gone. I retreated to the chaplain's office in shock and tried to quiet my mind. To my astonishment, I felt Linda's presence within me and heard her loving voice distinctly say, "Do not grieve for me. I am happy to be free of this body." Then I felt her leave, accompanied by a rush of energy out the top of my head.

I couldn't sleep that night. I felt as if I had witnessed, and in some way participated in, an inner rocket launch. I was on a high for several weeks until a huge wave of grief came crashing in. I was not grieving for her so much as for myself. Despite my glimpse through the veil of life and death, I experienced a terrible emotional emptiness in my heart that felt like a bottomless, dark crater. For months the grief came in waves with varying respites. An occasional sneaker wave would pull me completely under. I would toss and tumble in grief for hours until I was spit out, exhausted.

The following year, Christiane's visa was about to expire, requiring her to return to France. I was still deeply grieving Linda's death and knew that I was not emotionally ready to marry, yet circumstances required that I act. I trusted my inner knowing that my heart would eventually be more available. We got married sooner than I would have normally wanted. I am very grateful that I did. Christiane and I had a wonderful son, James, and a new chapter of my life unfolded as my heart gradually reopened to deeply love them both.

A Blind Man Sees

One of the most inspiring stories about trusting the heart and following inner guidance is found in Jacques Lusseyran's autobiography *And There Was Light*. This underground spiritual classic is still largely known by word of mouth. It deserves a much wider audience. Lusseyran, born in Paris in 1924 to a middle-class family, lost his sight in an accident at school when he was eight years old. At first he felt anguish and despair, but he soon realized he was looking at his situation in the wrong way. This was more than a simple insight—it was a revelation:

> At this point some instinct—I was almost about to say a hand laid on me—made me change course. I began to look more closely, not at things but at a world closer to myself, looking from an inner place to one further within, instead of clinging to the movement of sight toward the world outside.
>
> Immediately the substance of the universe drew together, redefined and peopled itself anew. I was aware of a radiance emanating from a place I knew nothing about, a place which might as well have been outside me as within. But radiance was there, or, to put it more precisely, light. It was a fact, for light was there.
>
> I felt incredible relief. Confidence and gratitude came as if a prayer had been answered. I found light and joy at the same moment, and I can say without hesitation that from that time on light and joy have never been separated in my experience. I have had them or lost them together.

Lusseyran's story is even more remarkable for what followed. He was seventeen when the Nazis invaded France and occupied Paris. Driven by an inner resolve from the core of his being, he became a major leader of the Resistance, organizing a group of over six hundred young men to clandestinely produce and distribute an anti-Nazi newspaper throughout France and to help downed airmen find safe passage to Spain.

Lusseyran, known as the Blind One, would personally vet each new member of his group in order to detect possible Nazi collaborators. He could read others with extraordinary accuracy and gained a reputation for being infallible. He was, however, ambivalent about only one member that he accepted. This man betrayed him and the entire leadership a year later. Lusseyran and his comrades were arrested by the Gestapo, interrogated, and shipped to Buchenwald. After nearly dying there, he became an informal spiritual counselor to many of the men because of his inner radiance. He was one of the few to survive.

We are all blind in a way until, like Lusseyran, we learn to "look from an inner place to one further within." It is one thing to discover this inner light, and it is another to let it guide us in our daily lives. For Lusseyran, this guidance took the form of great insight, courage, and compassion in the most demanding circumstances imaginable. Although he almost lost his life, he never lost his "sight," even in the depths of Nazi hell.

Self-Love and Self-Acceptance

Sometimes my spiritually oriented clients wonder whether self-love, self-acceptance, and self-care will reinforce the ego. They don't. Loving and accepting ourselves *as we are* allows us to step off the inner battle-field and to relax the knot of inner division.

Self-indulgence is different from self-care. Self-indulgence feeds the sense of being a separate self. When we become self-indulgent, our life is all about the little me. We don't really care about others or for the whole of life. Self-care means that we listen to our core needs, set reasonable boundaries with others, and live in balance. It also means that we question all of our limiting beliefs that create suffering for ourselves and others. And it means that we live in growing integrity with a deeper truth that we are not separate from anyone. Genuine self-care frees us to be more selfless.

Our basic needs are fairly simple—food, shelter, rest, health, human connection, and meaningful work. If we don't take basic care of ourselves, we are unable to really help anyone else, at least not for long. Burnout—becoming exhausted, sick, and resentful—is pointless. There are times when we need to stretch beyond our normal limits in order to be there for others or to meet a work commitment. At some point, however, we need to rest and replenish. The wisdom of the heart helps us to navigate these apparent dilemmas of when to say yes or no to the requests or demands of others. Sometimes a no will be the most wise and loving response in the long run, even if it temporarily disappoints someone. A no to someone else can be a yes to our inner truth.

Self-love and acceptance can easily begin as mental principles that transmute into ideals against which we judge ourselves. For example, we may think, "I *should* be more self-accepting." The judging mind is so tricky; it will use anything to point out what is wrong or missing and thus reinforce a core limiting belief. For this reason, sometimes it is not that helpful to encourage people to accept themselves. If they have a hard time doing so, they will feel like failures. Further, injunctions engender resistance. We don't like being told what to do, even if wisdom is being offered with the best of intentions.

I noted in chapter 4 that the conditioned mind only accepts conditionally. It is always bargaining along the lines of "If I accept this, maybe I can get rid of it." So rather than enjoining my clients and students to accept or love themselves more, I ask them if they can find that awareness in the heart that *already* loves and accepts them as they are.

EXPERIMENT *Self-Love and Self-Acceptance*

Find a quiet place, sit comfortably, and close your eyes. Bring your attention to your heart center. Take several slow, deep breaths and let your attention settle down and in.

Ask yourself: Is there something within me that loves and accepts me just as I am? Let the question go and be quiet.

Notice what happens in the area of your heart. If you can sense this place of self-love and acceptance, attune with it and let it in. Notice the impact as you do.

Then imagine embracing the part of you that feels unacceptable and unlovable in the center of your heart. Rest and breathe. Let the love saturate this part for several minutes.

(If you are unable to sense this place, ask yourself if there is a core belief about whether you are lovable and acceptable as you are. Then follow the experiment in chapter 4 about questioning core beliefs.) ●

We find unconditional acceptance in the depths of the heart. The deeper our attention goes, the more compassion and understanding we discover. It is as if there is a secret spring in the core of the heart. The Spanish poet Antonio Machado writes of this in his poem "Last Night as I Was Sleeping":

> Last night as I was sleeping,
> I dreamt—marvelous error!—
> that a spring was breaking
> out in my heart.
> I said: Along which secret aqueduct,
> Oh water, are you coming to me,
> water of a new life
> that I have never drunk?
>
> Last night as I was sleeping,
> I dreamt—marvelous error!—
> that I had a beehive
> here inside my heart.
> And the golden bees
> were making white combs
> and sweet honey
> from my old failures.
>
> Last night as I was sleeping,
> I dreamt—marvelous error!—
> that a fiery sun was giving
> light inside my heart.
> It was fiery because I felt
> warmth as from a hearth,
> and sun because it gave light
> and brought tears to my eyes.
>
> Last night as I slept,
> I dreamt—marvelous error!—
> that it was God I had
> here inside my heart.[1]

Soul: The Inner Sanctum

In chapter 2, I described three levels to the heart: ego, soul, and self. The egoic level is concerned with our self-image and its related feelings of pride, shame, self-esteem, and self-loathing. This level goes very deep, and much of our attention is ordinarily absorbed in maintaining an image acceptable to ourselves and others. The questions that arise from this level are: Do you see me? Am I okay? Do you like me? There is a natural desire and need to be accurately and appreciatively seen and to have what is seen reflected back to us—in psychological terms, to be mirrored. A certain amount of mirroring is necessary for attention to move beyond the self-image and self-story. Receiving it supports our self-trust and the ability to stand on our own.

My clients and students often report journeying through increasingly subtle layers of their hearts. As they do so, they discover why they closed their hearts and put up a series of barricades in the first place. Each wall is connected to an old emotional injury—a deep hurt due to abuse or neglect that was too much to bear at the time. Sometimes these walls appeared suddenly, and other times they appeared incrementally. They often arose without the person's conscious awareness, particularly if this happened in early childhood. It was easier and safer to shut down and armor the heart than to stay open and feel.

It takes courage and vulnerability to reopen these sensitive depths. Wounds to the heart are usually relational in origin, so the healing will often come through the loving acceptance and attunement of another person, be it a family member, friend, partner, or therapist. This process of healing takes time.

As the heart heals and clears, greater depths unfold. At some point, we may encounter what feels like a sacred core—what some call the soul. It is the place of greatest relational intimacy, whether we are relating as spiritual friends or lovers. Here the heart is undefended, innocent, and open. Each individual offers complete access to the other. It is a place of love, gratitude for life, compassion, appreciation, and joy. It is deeply touching to sit with people and experience their journey into this inner sanctum together.

Much of Rumi's poetry describes this depth of intimacy, which for him sprang out of the brief but extraordinarily transformative time he spent with his teacher Shams. Will Johnson, author of *Rumi: Gazing at the Beloved—The Radical Practice of Beholding the Divine*, offers the following poem, among others from Rumi, as evidence that Shams and Rumi spent most of their ninety days together gazing:

> If you want to know God,
> Then turn your face toward your friend,
> And don't look away.[2]

I have found that meditative gazing with an open friend or partner tends to evoke this soulful level of contact. A deep longing of the heart is fulfilled when this level of relational intimacy is touched. The taste of these sacred waters is extraordinarily sweet.

Gazing with a partner is a beautiful practice that I highly recommend. When meditatively gazing with someone, it is best to have no agenda and simply be open to what unfolds in the moment. It is never the same experience from session to session. You can go as long as you like, although thirty minutes is usually sufficient. Have a timer or clock nearby and find a space where you won't be interrupted. The intention with this practice is simply to be open to what unfolds within you and between you and your gazing partner.

EXPERIMENT   *Gazing with a Partner*

Sit comfortably across from your partner. Close your eyes for a minute and relax. Feel your feet on the floor, your breath, and your whole body.

Open your eyes and make relaxed, noneffortful eye contact. Allow your eyes to be soft and receptive. Be natural and at ease. This is not a staring contest. Feel free to blink, briefly close your eyes to rest, or adjust your posture as needed.

Stay at home in yourself and receive your partner. If you notice yourself being drawn into your partner's experience, gently recenter.

Be open and nonjudgmental. Don't try to hold onto or push away any experience. Silently notice what arises without trying to change it in any way.

Allow at least five minutes at the end to verbally share your experience with each other. ●

The Great Heart

As the heart opens and awakens, a universal, all-embracing love may emerge. When I interviewed my friend Dorothy Hunt, she described the awakening of her heart and the experience of this love:

> Sometime later, [there was] another awakening—of the heart. Deep tears of allowing life to enter the tabernacle of the Heart—a space once "reserved" for God. Now there was nothing that was not God. There was a sense of nectar flowing through the body—warm, sweet, loving presence, bathing in it, being overcome by love for everything and everyone. Seeing an arm, an eye, the skin, hearing music, birds singing—overwhelming love. Nothing was separate; nothing apart from love. Love beyond any description of love. Overwhelming love, overwhelming gratitude. Unsteadiness on the feet in the face of overwhelming love.

The heart area in the body is the portal to the Great Heart. Some of my clients and students have experienced the back of their heart area opening up into what feels like infinite space behind and around their bodies, as Kelly reported at the beginning of this chapter. It is as if there is a back door in the temple of the human heart that opens out to the cosmic heart. Only this Great Heart can fully embrace the collective suffering of humanity that is too much for an individual human heart to bear. As the heart fully flowers, we realize that we are all in this together, that the suffering of apparent others is also our suffering. It is the deep nature of the heart to reach out and embrace this suffering—to gather it into itself. Love is willing to go to hell.

One of my clients, Michele, recently experienced this Great Heart firsthand during a session of EMDR. Although she was raised in the Jewish faith, she grew up in a Catholic culture and felt an unlikely affinity with Jesus and Mary (although not the orthodox teachings of Christianity) throughout her life. At the end of our session, she was astonished at what had unfolded:

> I have trouble breathing; my lungs refuse to take in enough air. I look inside myself, and I am stunned to see my heart covered with gaping wounds flowing with immense grief. It's not my grief, but a grief gathered from each of us humans, a collective grief joined together in a dark river. I ache deep in my chest and bones. Sobs burst out of me while my body contorts and the dark flow increases. I don't want to escape but to fully meet this river of human sorrow and misery. I open to it as much as I can; my body trembles, my teeth chatter. The grief comes in waves, increasing. My heart stretches and stretches but still is not big enough to let it all pass through.
>
> I won't turn away but invite more. I welcome the unbearable because there is nothing else to do, nowhere else to go; this river must fully flow through my heart to free it.
>
> Suddenly, Christ's Heart appears in front of me, a couple of inches away, the river of all sorrows flowing through it. Our hearts get closer and closer. As if being pulled by a powerful magnet, my heart moves toward Jesus's Heart. Drawn from the inside by that mysterious force, it stretches even more, touches It and finally enters and melts in It.

Thorns are piercing my head and arms. I sense the rough wood of the cross against my body and the nails. It is as if I am being crucified.

I realize then that the pain of Christ on the cross was not all about the acute suffering of the body, being torn apart, the nails, the thorns, the wounds, but that it was the dark flow of mankind's suffering passing through His pure heart, filling it with grief, darkness, and ignorance. That pain was so much more immense and excruciating—a pain reaching from the four corners of the world, gathering the darkness of each one of our human hearts.

I do not know how, but I suddenly understand that all pains need to go there to start healing. None can be outside; not even the smallest fragment can be separated from that Heart. Pain needs to be unified to heal, and this is what Christ is doing. Unbelievably, I clearly experience the great love of Christ gathering all pain in Himself, unifying it, for ultimate redemption.

As the moment passes, I see that there is only One Heart in the whole world; it's so obvious, there are no separate hearts anywhere. That One Heart calls each of us to itself. I can hear it now and it is engulfing me through Christ's love.

The call of Christ's heart, by gathering all of humanity's darkness in itself, starts the ultimate healing, the sacred healing into truth. The Universal Heart is where all pain must go and where the darkness that envelops mankind must find it.

I tremble and sob; John holds my hands, and I plunge even deeper. The cross finishes its work of gathering pain through Blessed Jesus and His soul consumes the suffering harvested.

Then, finally, it is finished. I feel gratitude for the ending. What felt unbearable and sacrificial is over.

> The Cosmic Heart beats its beat, pulling and calling
> each individual heart to fully join and heal through
> the truth of unity.
>   I am dizzy and need to lie down while Oneness
> moves in me for a moment, and I see the dark shadow
> of a startled and rigid ego looking at it from out there.
> I am amazed.

In this remarkable session, Michele clearly tapped into the Great Heart that is able to gather in and transmute the collective suffering of humanity. It was almost unbearable, yet something in her felt compelled to experience it. This session marked a turning point for Michele, who is a highly sensitive person. She began to find her way out of a long period of intense darkness and suffering. I felt as if I had witnessed and participated in a sacred event.

Summary

Openheartedness is one of the most easily recognizable markers of inner knowing. The human heart is a keenly sensitive area of feeling and knowing that is a portal to our deepest self. Heart wisdom is a blend of deep feeling and understanding. Without discernment, love is easily blinded by desire. The heart area closes in the face of early emotional abuse and neglect, as well as in response to the normal challenges and stresses of daily life. It reopens when it is met with steady, attuned love. Self-acceptance, self-love, and self-care free us from our egocentricity and open us to the whole of life. The mind can only accept conditionally, but the heart accepts unconditionally. We do not need to *try* to love or accept ourselves; it is enough to attune with the love and acceptance that is already here.

As our attention deepens into the heart, subtler dimensions unfold. The deepest dimension of the human heart, sometimes called the soul, feels like a sacred temple. It is here that we experience the greatest human intimacy, love, compassion, and joy. The human heart opens into a nonlocalized Great Heart that is capable of embracing the suffering of humanity. Discovering and consciously living from both the Great Heart and the soulful depths of the human heart brings the deepest happiness as human beings.

Attuning with Openheartedness

Physically	Mentally	Emotionally	Energetically	Spiritually
Place your hand over the center of your chest and imagine that you are directly breathing into and from the depths of your heart area.	Inquire into any beliefs that obstruct your love and the acceptance of yourself and others.	Attune with that deep place in the heart that loves and accepts everything just as it is. Visualize embracing any parts of yourself that need this love. Hold them in your heart. Do the same for others—inwardly bless them and wish them well. Be generous in expressing your heartfelt love in daily life.	Sense into the various layers of your heart including the inner sanctum at the back of the heart. Sense into the opening behind the heart into the infinite or Great Heart.	Make a deep commitment to live openheartedly. Then work steadily and compassionately toward keeping it. Rest in and as the open heart. Gaze with a spiritually oriented friend.

8

spaciousness

Self-knowing awareness . . . is like pure space.
LONGCHENPA

One of my clients, Michelle Jeanne, wrote about sitting in silence after having a disturbing phone call:

I recently had a conversation with a dear old friend of mine. We were close friends in our teens and have kept in touch for the past forty years. During this telephone conversation, my friend spoke about how she had just ended a relationship with a friend of hers, due to judgments that had come up about one another. I became very emotional in the conversation and wondered if she might find some fault with me, making me the next person to be cut off from her life.

It would have been easy for me to leave it at that and to see my reaction in these terms. After all, I was afraid of being cut off. However, the depth of my emotion made me curious. There seemed to be more to it. So I decided to open up to those feelings and to rest there in the stillness.

As I did, it occurred to me that I have done the same thing in my own life. I have cut friends out of my life for the judgments that they carry. And it was painful to see this same behavior in myself. This deeper realization came to me because I stopped rationalizing, opened up, and allowed this insight to be revealed to me in the space of stillness.

We all have conversations where we feel disturbed by something that another person says, and our first reaction is self-defense. I know it well in myself. We continue an inner monologue criticizing the other or justifying our own position long after the outer conversation has ended. In this case, Michelle Jeanne's friend wasn't actually upset with her, but Michelle Jeanne feared that she could be cut off in a similarly abrupt way. As I noted in chapter 3, our radar is keenly attuned to these potential threats of abandonment.

Yet Michelle Jeanne suspected that her reaction involved more than the fear of being cut off. She wanted to be more in touch with what was really going on and decided to "rest . . . in the space of stillness." Her curiosity and love for the truth led her to slow down, feel, and be open. The realization that she had done the same thing that she feared—precipitously judged and cut off old friends—arose from the deep silence that she was able to tap into. The years she had devoted to living in the present moment and attuning with an inner spacious silence allowed her to soften her defenses and be vulnerable enough to explore her own reactions. As a result, she had a transformative insight.

Spaciousness is the last of the four major somatic markers of inner knowing. When we get in touch with our inner knowing, there is often a sense of vast space within and around our bodies, and this subjective sense of space is almost always accompanied by a deep silence. Genuine openness is very still. This spacious silence is always present in the heart of any experience. No matter how busy or stimulated we may be, there is an inner silent spaciousness that coexists, awaiting our discovery. If we slow down enough, we can sense it. As we attune with it our lives transform, as Michelle Jeanne's has and continues to.

Discovering Inner Space: Open-mindedness

The sense of inner space grows stronger as we are less identified with our thinking. In chapter 4, I invited you to witness thoughts as if they were clouds passing through an open sky. If you like, take a few minutes to explore this experiment again. Just observe the process of thoughts coming and going. Don't invest any of them with special significance. What do you notice?

If you don't buy into them and simply observe them, you will probably feel some space around them, as if you were now noticing the sky behind and around the clouds. The more you practice this, the stronger this sense of space becomes. Awareness is often likened to the sky or to space. When we believe our thoughts, it is hard to sense this space. Our attention is trapped inside of them like an airplane going through a cloudbank.

If a thought is very compelling, this process of neutral observation will be more challenging. Our belief in a thought makes us identify with it; believe one, and it is yours! The willingness to question and see through thought is like letting a breeze pass through an open window. Thoughts are sometimes quite useful; however, our identification with them is not.

Belief in thought is like fuel in a car. The less we believe that our thoughts are us, the less power they have to drive our lives. Long-standing patterns of thought—those rooted in childhood—will take time to taper off. It can take a while for the brain to rewire itself. Along the way we can see thoughts for what they are—just thoughts—and be less burdened by them. My friend Dorothy Hunt, whom I quoted in chapter 7, described her experience of the mind:

> Whenever the mind is not engaged, a sense of vast, expansive space is experienced. Even when the mind is engaged in thought, something is still open to the experience of thought; it is not bothered by the mind nor does it take its thought very seriously. There is the experience of stillness inside regardless of experience.

My clients find it easier to observe some thoughts more than others. Those thoughts that carry a strong emotional charge are the hardest to feel space around. Beliefs that induce shame or terror are particularly challenging; they exert a strong gravitational pull to identify with them. We cling to our familiar inner maps with surprising tenacity, even if they cause us to suffer.

When someone is very convinced of a core limiting belief and is unable to feel any space around it, I will sometimes ask, "If you can't disbelieve your harsh self-judgment, would you be willing to at least suspend a conclusion? Are you willing to *not know* if it is true or not?" Usually they are willing. Ask yourself if you are willing to suspend your conclusions, especially with troubling judgments.

An open mind—one that is willing to not know—fosters a sense of space. I love looking at the ancient maps of the seas with their vaguely drawn continents and vast open spaces. Imagine what it must have been like to sail out into such an unknown world five centuries ago. Even as the maps of our planet, solar system, galaxy, and universe have become increasingly precise in the twenty-first century, we continue to live in a universe that is largely unknown. Respected theoretical physicists suggest that the universe may be made up of as yet undetected, vibrating "superstrings" with multiple coexisting dimensions, not to mention mysterious "dark energy." No one knows with certainty what this world is really made of. As much data as we gather about the physical universe, we will always live in an open-ended mystery. The horizon of knowledge is always widening. When we acknowledge that we don't know and can never know everything, a different kind of knowing becomes available—one that is much more attuned with our body and with how life is unfolding in the moment.

Discovering Inner Space: Open-Bodiedness

Identifying with our body—mistaking it for our self—obscures the sense of inner space even more than identifying with our thoughts does. Just as open-mindedness allows for a greater sense of space, so, too, does an *open-bodiedness*—the feeling of openness in and around the body. I wonder if this unusual term might ever enter ordinary usage, such as, "Have you met Lucy? She has a wonderful, open-bodied approach to life." Or perhaps the opposite: "Yes, I agree, Darren was not very open-bodied to the new change when we talked about it." Although it sounds strange to the ear now, who knows a century from now?

While the term *open-bodied* is not important, the experience of feeling open space in and around the body is. Most of us don't pay a lot of attention to the sensations inside our bodies unless we are hungry, injured, or ill. We tend to see our body as something very solid and dense. Yet, as we have learned from Dan Siegel's description of interoception in chapter 1 and Eugene Gendlin's discovery of felt sensing, described in chapter 2, our bodies have a tremendous native sensitivity and intelligence. As we discover the value of tuning into the interior of our body, we also begin to realize that our body is not as solid as we imagine. It is, in fact, filled with space.

To discover this space, it helps to close your eyes and sense into your body. Allow fifteen minutes for the following experiment and take your time with each step.

EXPERIMENT *Sensing Space in the Body*

Find a quiet place to sit comfortably and close your eyes. Take a few deep breaths and let your attention settle down and into your body.

Feel the palms of your hands and notice a sense of energy radiating out from them. Allow the sense of your hands to expand so that they feel lighter and more spacious, as if you are wearing large energy gloves.

Do the same thing with the soles of your feet—feeling their sensitivity and expansion.

Let this sense of space and energy in your hands and feet spread up your arms and legs.

Take your time to sense this growing feeling of alive space in all of your limbs.

Feel it spread into your shoulders,
to your hips,
to your upper back and chest,
to your lower back and belly,
and then throughout your torso.
Sense this space in your neck,
your jaw,
your mouth,
your cheeks,
your eyes,
your ears,
and your forehead and scalp.
Feel it in both hemispheres of your brain.
Sense it throughout your entire body as a whole—an open,
alive spaciousness.

Take a few minutes to be with this feeling of inner space.

When you are ready, slowly open your eyes and retain the feeling
of space. Notice what happens to your sense of the environment.
Does it seem as solid as it did before this experiment?

When you drop the image of your body and just sense it as it is, it feels
less defined—more like a diffuse cloud than a solid object. In this way
it is similar to a thought passing through the sky of awareness. It is
harder to sense its borders when your eyes are closed. This spaciousness can be a little disorienting to your sense of self, since your body
serves as a kind of ground for your personal identity. You may also
feel bored by the lack of visual stimulation, get lost in your thoughts,
or tend to doze off while focusing on it. If you stay with this sense of
inner space, however, it will deepen and expand. You will realize that
your body is like a huge cathedral filled with space.

"When I'm in my truth, I feel as if I have really taken space up in my
body, like somehow it expands inside," said Silke Greiner. "It's almost
as if I get bigger."

As you explore this sense of space more deeply, you will begin
to realize that it is not confined to the interior of the body but also

surrounds it. When you try to find a boundary, you can't. This leads us to the second experiment in experiencing space.

EXPERIMENT *Sensing Space Around the Body*

Repeat the steps in the previous experiment, this time a little more quickly.

As you feel a clear sense of space within your body, also begin to sense space around your body.

Feel into the space in front of your body. Imagine you are inhaling from it and exhaling out into it. Notice how far this space seems to extend with your exhalation. Physical objects cannot obstruct it. Is there any boundary or limit to it?

Feel into the space behind your body, breathing from and into it. Take your time here. This is less familiar territory. Again notice if there is any boundary or limit.

Feel the space on the left side of your body, breathing and noticing if there is a boundary.

Feel the space on the right side of your body, breathing and noticing if there is a boundary.

Feel the space above your body, into the heavens, and then below, deep into the ground.

Feel the space all around you and rest in it. ◉

As you become more familiar with this exploration, you will begin to realize that not only is there space within you but also that *you are in an infinite space.* It is like a fish that suddenly discovers it has been unknowingly swimming in the ocean.

The final step is very simple and does not require an additional exercise: as you rest *in* this infinite space, simply *be* it. Don't take yourself as a localized object. When this happens, another shift in identity occurs. It feels like your body is *inside* of you as spacious awareness.

A tremendous freedom accompanies this sense of being infinite space. This is equivalent to the background that I described in chapter 5. We no longer feel bounded by the mind or the body, even as they continue to operate normally. We are able to intimately witness our lives. Several of the people that I interviewed described experiencing this.

"It feels as if I am made of clear empty space that is sentient all the way through the internal space of my body," wrote my colleague Judith Blackstone. "Yes, spacious, open, expansive, vast—made of space and everything else made of space."

"It is a sense of boundlessness, no boundary—really you could say not having a body at all. Certainly not being a body. More like being this space, which is really empty space which is the substance of everything," said my friend Stephan Bodian, adding, "I know that it sounds abstract, but it's an energetic experience."

When I interviewed my friend Rick Hanson about his inner sense of knowing, he first chose the example of knowing without doubt that his wife loved him. He described sensing a relaxation and stability in the heart and belly areas, a lack of contraction, and "a sense of space—an opening all around." He contrasted this with the sense that accompanied knowing the mathematical formula for the volume of a sphere, which felt to him more mental and localized in the head. Then I asked him about his sense of the one who knows—awareness itself.

"It is really hard to describe. It's almost visual," he said. "I know it's not vast space, it's *like* vast, empty space. The Dzogchen masters say this: it's beyond any label. It is like the vast space knows."

He went on to describe a kind of impersonal gratitude that also arose:

Rick: The knowing has a tonal quality of impersonality . . . [and] bows to what is magnificent, pure, and simple, "Wow, thank you!"

JP: Gratitude?

Rick: Yes. That's very beautiful. There are markers to deep knowing. Real insight is coupled with relief, gratitude, and release. That's one of the markers of the absolute.

We can recognize several of the markers of inner knowing in Rick's description—spaciousness, gratitude (openheartedness), and relief and release (core relaxation and letting go).

Several people I interviewed described a background space that began to open as they deepened in their inner knowing.

"It's like an expansive vastness that I feel in my back space, almost as if I'm being very gently pulled or drawn toward my back space," said Debira Branscombe. "I almost feel it in the shoulder blades. . . . There's this being quality to it, being truth."

For Lily Sun, one of my graduate students, this sense of background spaciousness first appeared relationally when she felt a sunlike awareness emerge behind herself and the person with whom she was sitting. The intimate and silent quality of it frightened her at first.

> Lily: The image is of an eclipse. It does feel like all of a sudden I'm the moon, the sun is behind me, and when I fall into the space, the sensation I get is that I'm seeing the person—the planet—and then there's the sun behind it. It feels like it's bigger and more powerful in a lot of ways than just this planet.

> JP: So the sun is behind you and behind the other?

> Lily: Yes. When I first dropped into it, it was relational, and it was frightening because I had never experienced it—this type of connection. It was a really wordless space.

> JP: How does your sensing change from this larger space?

> Lily: It's not as personal. It's odd. (She chuckles.) There's a timeless quality. There's a knowing that's not just within myself. . . . I feel more in my divine self, if that's the right word. . . . There's this open—I can't quite say solid—there's this open, present quality to it.

For Lily, this background spacious awareness appeared like a sun in herself and, simultaneously, in the other. The planet of the little me, a moon, was eclipsed by the sun of awareness. The shift of attention into the space behind was accompanied by a profound silence and a new and initially frightening level of intimacy that felt less personal. We usually equate closeness, connection, and intimacy with being more personal, but Lily was having a different experience that was hard to put into words. Was it divine? It was certainly very open and present.

I resonated with Lily's novel description of her experience because it paralleled my own. When something similar first began to emerge as I sat with some of my clients years ago, I experienced it as a "wrap-around space." It feels like the same open, spacious awareness looking out through *these* eyes is also wrapping around and seeing through *those* eyes.

The other week I was sitting across from Bob Henson, a member of one of my inquiry groups, peacefully gazing in silence for a few minutes as part of an exercise. At one point his eyes lit up with amazement. When we took a few minutes to share at the end, he said that the sense of separation had completely dissolved. He realized that it was the same awareness looking out from both of us. It was a revelation, one he had read about but never directly experienced. He was brimming with delight and awe.

Spacious or Spacy?

There is a difference between being spacious and being spacy. To be spacious is to be open, available, and receptive. It arises from seeing through our limited identity. It is not reacting to or pushing away anything. When we feel spacious, we are also very present and grounded in the body. Spaciousness is accompanied by a natural detachment—we make our best effort and are able to let go.

Spaciness, on the other hand, is a reaction against something. It is a refusal to be present, an avoidance of direct experience. It can take subtle forms, such as daydreaming when we feel bored, or more dramatic forms, such as dissociation when we have gone through a trauma. When we are spacy, we don't feel all here. We are not fully

SPACIOUSNESS

in our bodies. We feel distracted, disengaged, ungrounded, and not very present. Spaciness is dissociative rather than detached. If you are feeling a little spacy, it is good to ask yourself, "What am I avoiding?" Facing whatever we are avoiding, whether it is an inner feeling such as fear or shame or a challenging outer situation, may temporarily provoke anxiety, but it will eventually be grounding. In this way, spaciness becomes a portal to spaciousness, a theme we explored in chapter 3.

Spacious Intimacy

I want to make a subtle but important point: we do not create a sense of space; we attune with it. The mind cannot manufacture spacelike awareness because it is already here. It is who we already are. It quietly awaits our conscious discovery. The sense of space grows stronger the less we believe that we are limited to our minds and bodies.

The sense of spacious awareness is also contagious. As you read or hear other people's descriptions of it, something within you may light up in recognition. We can experience it when we are reading a book that is written from this awareness, and we can certainly feel it when we are in the presence of someone who has discovered it in themselves. For me, simply being in the presence of my two main teachers, Jean Klein and Adyashanti, regardless of their verbal teachings (as valuable as they are), was a major catalyst for realizing this spacious awareness. The beauty is that this space doesn't belong to anyone, yet it is shared by everyone, knowingly or unknowingly.

Our lives change as we feel more of a sense of space within and around us. We become more intimate with our experience and, at the same time, less attached to outcomes. I have come to think of this as *spacious intimacy.* We are available to intimately experience and welcome what is here without becoming lost in it. Here is how Walt Whitman, not one to lack passion, described it in his poem "Song of Myself":

Apart from the pulling and hauling stands what I am,
Stands amused, complacent, compassionating, idle, unitary,
Looks down, is erect, or bends an arm on an impalpable certain rest,

> Looking with side-curved head curious what will come next,
> Both in and out of the game and watching and wondering at it.[1]

I love "compassionating"—another useful word to add to our vocabulary. Yet what I love most in this excerpt from Whitman's epic poem is the phrase "both in and out of the game." He is above his life, looking down, compassionate, bemused, relaxed, and curious. And he is fully engaged. He is not a remote witness, dryly disengaged—a pit some long-term meditators fall into after spending years on their zafus watching their thoughts. He is on both the outside and the inside of his life—spacious and intimate.

Adyashanti describes this perspective as "witnessing from the inside." We are very close to our experience—in the very center of it, actually—without being lost in it. This does not mean that we are free of internal reactions—I doubt this ever happens completely, given the nature of conditioning—but we become increasingly available to be with them, accepting them as they are with curiosity and affection. Something deep within each of us, this spacious awareness, is welcoming our reactions just as they are. What a blessing!

This sense of spacious intimacy also applies to our relationships with others and to life in general. Over the past decade, I have felt increasingly like an affectionate anthropologist or sociologist as I witness our collective human suffering and struggle to find happiness. As I read or listen to the news, I find myself thinking, "Yes, this is what we do as humans. We fight wars over ideas, resist facing reality, idealize and devalue one another, are egocentric and tribal, *and* we are curious, loving, sensitive, intelligent, and sometimes courageous beings trying to survive and make sense out of very challenging circumstances." This orientation is an interesting blend of an increasingly objective observation coupled with deep compassion. There is a strong desire to help alleviate suffering and the knowledge that in the end it is an inside job for everyone.

There is an important distinction between intimacy and merging. To be intimate means to be very close, familiar, or friendly with someone or something. Spacious intimacy refers to an *essential* closeness. In regard to people, we know the apparent other as an expression of our deepest nature as spacious awareness. They are not essentially separate from us, even as they are clearly distinct. It sounds paradoxical, but it is a question of levels. We feel a shared ground with others and, at the same time, acknowledge and even celebrate their diverse, individuated form. Metaphorically, the same ocean gives rise to countless unique waves. True intimacy requires autonomy. We are able to be very close *and* to stand on our own. This is not something that the ego can do.

Merging happens when we are undifferentiated from the other person on the level of form. We lose touch with our own thoughts, feelings, needs, and experiences in order to feel close to another person or to avoid conflict. It happens all the time, almost always when we are children, but also with surprising frequency as adults. If we are feeling consistently resentful about giving too much to someone we are close to, we are probably in a merged relationship. So, too, if we are unable to know how we really feel or what we need. Merging requires the loss of autonomy. I will explore these themes of intimacy and autonomy more thoroughly in chapter 10.

Summary

A sense of spaciousness is a common marker of our inner knowing. In addition to feeling grounded, aligned, and openhearted, we often feel spacious when we are in touch with our deeper self. We can sense space in our minds and our bodies. As we learn to witness our thoughts like clouds passing through the sky and to disbelieve, or at least suspend, conclusions about their truth, we become more aware of a silent inner space. Likewise, as we intimately sense into our bodies, we will discover a profound sense of spaciousness inside and all around us. Our body is not the dense physical object that we take it to be. At some point we may recognize that not only are we immersed in infinite space, but we also *are* it.

As we attune with the sense of open space within and around us, we carry this into our daily life and our contact with others. Doing so brings the experience of spacious intimacy. We can begin to directly sense the shared ground and space with our fellow beings even as we acknowledge and appreciate our differences. Spaciousness, which is open, receptive, and grounded, is different from spaciness, which is avoidant, disengaged, and ungrounded.

Attuning with Spaciousness

Physically	Mentally	Emotionally	Energetically	Spiritually
Spend time outdoors and contemplate the infinite expanse of the sky.	Observe all of your thoughts as if they were clouds passing through the sky.	Notice the sense of interior space when you feel love, gratitude, and joy.	Sense into the space that permeates your body.	Realize that who you really are is not bounded by any thought, feeling, or sensation.
Relax in the prone position, close your eyes, and surrender the weight of your body to the earth. Sense the openness within and around your body.	Question all of your core limiting beliefs and be willing to suspend conclusion about the ones that you cannot yet see through.		Sense into the infinite space within which your body is immersed. Be this open, infinite space.	

PART IV

the fruits of inner knowing

As the noise of our conditioned body-mind lessens
and we are better able to hear the signals of our inner
knowing, our life comes into accord with a deeper
current. Clear inner guidance helps us to navigate
the challenges of our daily life more gracefully. Yet the
essential bodily markers—a relaxed groundedness,
inner alignment, openheartedness, and
spaciousness—point us to something still
more profound, our true nature.

9

self-recognition

We cannot understand, love, and welcome others
without first knowing and loving ourselves.

JEAN KLEIN

At the opening of part 3, I shared a story of how I once found cairns—those improvised piles of stone left by hikers—in the High Sierras, marking the way across a granite ridge to a hidden trailhead. Like Sierras hikers, we all are on a kind of journey, and the somatic markers of inner knowing, like cairns, are one way to know that we are on the right track. On track toward what, though? Where are the markers of inner bodily knowing leading us? As "right" as these subtle somatic qualities feel, they are not ends in themselves; they are homing signals. As we feel ourselves more deeply relaxed and grounded, inwardly aligned, openhearted, and spacious, we are honing in on a deeper truth—the truth of who we really are.

Our body's deep sensitivity is calling us home. Yet home is not somewhere, some when, or something other than what is already wholly present now. Our true nature is not some inner state that will be found in the future. It is always here and now, unbounded by space or time. It can never be objectified. Further, the heart of the one who is looking—the apparent separate self—is what is being looked for. Nisargadatta Maharaj said it most succinctly: "The seeker is the sought."

This wisdom teaching is very puzzling for the linear mind that thinks in terms of someone attaining something. A student of the Indian sage Ramana Maharshi once asked for help to find his true nature. "You are like a man standing in his living room, asking how to get home," Ramana replied. We are already home—we just don't realize it. Infinite awareness is shining through your eyes as you read this—you are not who you *think* you are. Take a moment to open to this possibility.

Our body's inner knowing is pointing us toward this self-recognition. Certainly being relaxed, grounded, aligned, spacious, and openhearted makes day-to-day living much easier, but there is a deeper invitation at work within each of us—to wake up. Self-recognition and awakening are different ways of describing the same thing. At some point we realize that we are not the limited being that we consciously and subconsciously take ourselves to be. We see that none of our stories and images about ourselves are actually true. This initial recognition can feel as if the clouds have briefly parted, revealing a vast, open space.

When this happens, the veil of personal identity temporarily lifts, and we know ourselves as open, awake awareness. We are in touch with our natural lucidity. In rare instances this awakeness is sustained after the first contact. In most cases, however, the conditioned body-mind reasserts itself, and there is a return to one's familiar identity. Yet a taste of this homecoming remains. It is like someone who briefly awakens from a dream and then falls asleep again; the wakefulness is never completely forgotten. It continues to vibrate on the periphery of the dream, in the background of who we imagine ourselves to be. Our lives start to reorient around this clearer sense of who we really are.

As a result, we may begin to slow down and start paying attention to our actual experience. We may tune in to the sensations of our body or start to notice moments of silence between thoughts. We may question our limiting beliefs and emotional reactions and become interested in the process of how we bind and blind ourselves. Or, as

Adyashanti puts it, we become interested in "the pitfalls and cul-de-sacs that un-enlighten us along the journey."

"How do I unenlighten myself?" is a subtly different question from "How do I awaken?" The former presumes that we are obscuring a natural wakefulness that is already here. Rather than wondering how we *get there,* we can inquire, "Is it true that what I seek is not already here?" I invite you to sit with these questions and feel what they evoke. Something in you will respond if you don't go to your thinking mind for an answer.

Awakening does not come from moving forward, but from falling back. It is a letting go into the unknown. In Zen it is called "the backward step." We start to track our experience backward. For instance, you can evoke the sense of "I am" and then follow it back to its source—a classic form of self-inquiry. What happens if you focus your attention on the thought "I am"? Can you sense where and how it localizes in your body? If you follow it inward, where does it draw your attention? Or you can feel the deep yearning of the heart to come home and follow that yearning back. These kinds of intuitive inquiries lead us out of the certitude of the conditioned mind into the unfamiliar territory of "I don't know."

The mind may think that "I don't know" is the wrong answer to the question "Who or what am I?" Yet, in fact, "I don't know" is the most accurate and honest answer. When we deeply investigate all of our placeholder identities, such as being a man or a woman, an American or a German, a white, a brown, or a black, a hetero- or homosexual, they fall to the side like name tags scattered on the floor at the end of a convention. The simple truth is that we actually don't know who we are. Gradually we learn to relax into this not knowing. As Jean Klein once told me during a private interview, "Abide in the heart, not knowing."

At some point, having made ourselves available, we are taken by grace. This taking may be sudden and clearly recognizable or slow and barely noticed—a waterfall or a broad river gently meeting the ocean. Whether sudden or gradual, there is a gravitational shift of identity from form to formless, from being someone to being no one, from being an object bounded by time and space to being open, awake, and infinite awareness. There is clarity, with no one left to claim it as his or her own. It marks the beginning of a new chapter of life.

Presence and Present-Centeredness

As we discover who we really are, there is a natural presence that unfolds like the fragrance from a blossom. I think of it as the radiance of being. It is completely uncontrived and spontaneous. It is also gently contagious. I remember sensing it with both of my main teachers, Jean Klein and Adyashanti, even though they had completely different personalities, backgrounds, and teaching styles. The first time that I met each of them, I immediately dropped into a deep, vibrant silence. What was wakeful in me could sense it in them. None of this was mediated by thought.

Some spiritual traditions call this phenomenon "transmission," implying that something is being given or transmitted. Certain energies can be willfully directed, but this is not what was happening when I sat with my teachers. They were simply *being* themselves. I was just sitting in their presence without any direct visual or verbal contact.

Transmission is actually resonance. The truth of who we are resonates with itself in others. Being shines through a particular being and invites itself into the foreground of awareness in other beings. The most important sharing happens in silence. Words are secondary, mainly helping the mind to see its limits and to relax. An effective outer teacher points students to their own inner teacher. There is really only one teacher—our inner knowing.

There is a meaningful distinction between *present-centered* and *presence* that is often overlooked. The former can be a doorway to the latter, but this is not always the case. Being present-centered means focusing attention on present experience. For example, right now I am aware of the sound of a passing car, the contact between my body and the chair that I am sitting in, the afternoon light outside my study, my breath, a feeling of quiet contentment, and a sense of wonder about what thoughts and words are about to appear. In other words, I am aware of sensations, feelings, and thoughts; these are the *contents* of awareness.

Presence refers to the recognition of awareness itself, to the *context* of experience rather than the content. This spacelike awareness feels open, awake, and full of potential. There is a sense of being—not being anyone in particular, just being. Within this presence there are fluctuating degrees of present-centered attention, like waves on the ocean. The waves can be in different states—sometimes very calm, as is the case for me right now, and sometimes rather choppy and fragmented, for example, when I am distracted and not really paying full attention to what is going on in front of my nose. (My wife is good at pointing out the latter moments, which is both humorous and humbling.) Regardless of what is happening on the level of present experience, there is an awareness of an openness within which it is happening.

The distinction between presence and present-centeredness affects how we understand and approach spiritual practice. Some traditions insist that the mind must first learn to focus and be quiet before a deeper realization of one's true nature can happen. From this perspective, students who are advised to "rest in and as open awareness" without having first learned how to focus their attention on an object such as the breath or a mantra will spend the vast majority of their time daydreaming or restlessly fidgeting.

There is some truth to this observation. I have been on long retreats where some participants report experiencing this restlessness. In my own case, I spent nearly ten years doing a mantra meditation that served as a subtle anchor for attention. Later, when I adopted a practice of simply resting in silence, it was an easy and liberating transition. The preceding years of subtly focusing attention may have helped. It is hard to know. Some people don't seem to need this prior training. For others, a regular sitting meditation practice can be quite lovely and beneficial. For yet others, meditating on an object can become an obstacle over time, leading to a feeling of inner dryness. You have to find what is true for you.

If you are interested in a sitting meditation practice, try it and see how it goes. If you have difficulty simply resting in silence, you may want to begin the meditation with a focus of attention, such as the breath in the lower belly (hara) or the heart center. As the mind becomes quieter while you sit, experiment with letting the focus go and resting in awareness.

Presence is not cultivated; it is uncovered. In rare cases this uncovering can be sudden and quite dramatic. Sometimes an extreme health or relational crisis will trigger a sudden letting go and opening when someone has had absolutely no spiritual background or practice. Byron Katie is a great example of someone who experienced this sudden uncovering.[1] These kinds of openings initially tend to be accompanied by lots of inner and outer upheaval. Generally speaking, the more balanced and integrated the body-mind is, the easier it is to rest in and as simple awareness. Yet there are no preconditions for recognizing who we are; there don't seem to be any hard and fast rules.

We can be relatively present-centered without being aware of presence. And we can be aware of presence without being particularly present-centered. They are different domains. That said, present-centered attention is a common portal to self-recognition and presence. In any case, it is always useful to pay attention.

Self-Trust, Inner Authority, and Autonomy

When we are willing to not know who we are and to free ourselves from the cage of the conditioned mind, a different kind of knowing emerges, one that is more heartfelt and whole-bodied. While this more direct, moment-to-moment way of knowing does not confer omniscience, it does allow us to be more in touch with ourselves and to grow in self-trust, inner authority, and autonomy.

Self-trust is difficult as long as we identify with the critical intellect. This was certainly true in my case. I struggled with self-doubt even after having many years of meditation and wisdom teachings under my belt. This shifted when I attended my first weeklong retreat with Jean Klein in 1986 in the mountains south of Santa Cruz, along the California coast. In the mornings, in a room overlooking redwood groves and the Monterey Bay, Jean would lead the group in what he called his "body approach"—a very slow and gentle form of yoga that emphasized sensing the body's subtle energy and spaciousness. In those days, he would walk among us, quietly observing and, more rarely, making small corrections to our posture. At one point, as I did a seated twist, I could sense him standing behind me. I then felt the slight upward brush of his finger behind my heart center. To my surprise, I spontaneously visualized a vertical line running along my spine and the repair of an inner, unknown fracture in my heart. That night I dreamed that I pulled out of one of my ears a large worm that had burrowed deep in my brain. As I did, I *knew* that this disgusting parasite was my self-doubt. I also knew that Jean's gentle touch had somehow facilitated its release.

This was a turning point in developing self-trust. Before it, I was prone to self-doubt and continually questioning the validity of my direct experience. If there were periods of inner peace and joy or moments of genuine insight and openness, afterward I would wonder whether they were real or just fabrications of my mind. I was deeply identified with the judging mind that relentlessly questioned everything, including my direct experience. While my self-doubt didn't change overnight after this experience, I began to see my doubt more clearly for what it was—a distorted lens through which I viewed myself and the world. In a certain way, I began to doubt my doubt and to trust the knowing of my heart.

The conditioned mind is always strategizing, seeking to avoid pain and to increase pleasure. It is driven by fear and desire. This is its job. In contrast, our inner knowing is interested in the truth—how things actually are. It has no agenda to survive, fit in, be admired, or to feel better. It is concerned with love, wisdom, integrity, and being in service to the whole of life.

As we learn to slow down, tune in to our inner guidance, and act on it, our self-trust grows. We increasingly get the feel for when something resonates as being true or false for us, in or out of accord. This sense of inner resonance becomes our inner authority. We gradually wean ourselves from convention and learn to think and feel for ourselves. We withdraw the projection of authority onto others as we recognize it in ourselves. As a result, we are less likely to follow outer authorities unless it is clear that they are in touch with a deep authority within themselves. Our self-trust comes from the felt sense of this inner authority.

Trusting our inner authority brings spiritual autonomy, the ability for true self-governance. It is the entrance into real adulthood. We are willing and able to stand on our own. Yet this inner freedom and independence is not egocentric or disconnected from others. As we trust our inner authority more, we are less defensive and more available to meet and love life as it is. Our autonomy is not based upon some ideology or need to be right. It does not take a rigid position. True autonomy adapts to the revelation of new facts and insights.

Some of my clients and students occasionally express ambivalence about trusting their inner authority because they fear the loss of connection with others. There is a deep fear of isolation and aloneness. Yet the fear of aloneness is rooted in our belief that we are a separate self. Abdicating our authority and merging with others only masks this underlying fear of aloneness and isolation. As we learn to trust who we really are and not who we think we are, we discover that we are not essentially separate from anyone. We are unique, free, and unimaginably interconnected. The recognition of our true inner autonomy allows us to enjoy our human interdependence. As we grow in self-trust, we can give and receive that much more freely. It is a joy to do so.

Embodiment

I suggested earlier that self-recognition or awakening is the beginning of a new chapter of life, one that could be entitled "Embodiment." It is one thing to realize our infinite nature on the level of the mind; it is another to do so on the level of feelings and sensations. This is a more challenging process because emotional and instinctual conditioning runs far more deeply than mental conditioning. We can be disidentified from our mental stories and images and continue to be very identified with our emotional and instinctual patterns, which we unconsciously act out. There may be a sizable gap between our inner realization and the way that we lead our daily lives, depending upon our conditioning and the psychological work we have already done on ourselves. It is a question of congruence. How aligned is our living with our knowing?

If we remain open, the process of *waking up* from form and realizing that we are no one and no thing is followed by a process of *waking down* into form. It is wonderful to know and to experience that we are not bounded by anything, yet it is a negative freedom—a freedom *from*. We are still residing in a subtle state of separation from all that we are free of. There is still a knower and a known. But what remains, if not oneself? Are we free to fully enter into form, particularly this body?

Spiritual traditions with an imbalanced transcendental and masculine emphasis stop here, either devaluing or entirely dismissing emotions and the body. After all, once you know yourself as the infinite, why bother with the finite? As I noted in my discussion of mental bypassing in chapter 3, our understanding of what spirit is will influence our response to this question. If we see spirit as only being transcendent and formless, we will want to dwell there. If we understand that spirit is both transcendent *and* immanent, we will want to discover and live it in our ordinary life. The consequences of our view are huge.

Our body is form par excellence. As Jean Klein noted, it is our "nearest environment." The more clearly we sense that our body is an expression of pure awareness, the more deeply we sense this of the world. There is a direct correspondence: as we are with our body, so we are with the world. As the true nature of the body is discovered, the world becomes an increasingly transparent expression of consciousness.

My friend Rupert Spira describes this transformational process as awareness colonizing the body.[2] Awareness saturates the conditioned body. Deeper levels take more time to touch and transform. For me, awake awareness has been spontaneously, relentlessly, and sometimes arduously drilling down through the bedrock of conditioning for the last decade. As this process continues and deepens, lingering distinctions between knower and known dissolve. Only knowing remains, and a great intimacy begins to reveal itself.

10

the great intimacy

We shall not cease from exploration, and the
end of our exploring will be to arrive where we
started and know the place for the first time.

T. S. ELIOT

Where do we most deeply meet one another?

I had never carefully considered this question until some years ago, when one of my clients said something that sparked a revelation. She had felt very isolated her entire life and found it hard to trust anyone, myself included. One day, out of the blue, she said, "I have never met anyone outside of myself." She was trying to describe how isolated she felt—how she could not contact others beyond her shame and fear-bound sense of self. I completely misunderstood her and took her to mean that all meetings happen within the unbounded self. Talk about an empathic failure! When I shared my excitement about the depth of her insight, she corrected me, and after some initial confusion we had a good laugh. Nonetheless, I had accidently gained a seminal insight into relationships.

Before this, I had always assumed that I met others somewhere outside of myself. It seemed that I had to extend myself to connect with someone else. It might be with a handshake, eye contact, or an exchange of words. I am here, you are there, and we meet somewhere in between as we reach out to each other, testing the waters. Psychologists call this the intersubjective field.

We all know this experience and its many variations as we encounter family members, lovers, friends, colleagues, acquaintances, and strangers. Each relationship has varying degrees of closeness depending upon our mutual resonance, roles, attraction, familiarity, and trust. They also happen on different levels—physical, emotional, mental, energetic, and spiritual. Subtle and complex bonds form over time based upon these interactions. They can be nurturing, ambivalent, indifferent, or destructive. Some are short-term and volatile; others are long-term and relatively stable. All of them change.

We also form bonds with everything else on the planet—animals, environments, physical objects, and especially ideas. As earthlings, we are made of stardust and share the same oxygen with all of the creatures on this small, precious blue sphere. Manifest life is an infinitely complex web of relationships. As the wilderness sage and early ecologist John Muir observed, "When we try to pick out anything by itself, we find it hitched to everything else in the universe."

EXPERIMENT *Inquiry into Essential Meeting*

When have you felt the deepest contact and connection with another being? Where does this most intimate and essential meeting occur? What do you experience right now as you inquire? Take some time to reflect on these questions. ◉

My accidental revelation crystallized the conscious understanding of something that I was already experiencing. As I sat with this insight about essential meeting, I realized that it always happens when I fully, effortlessly *receive* the other within myself. I saw that I never had to leave myself to connect with someone else. Yes, I needed to open, but I did not need to go anywhere. It is a subtle but important insight. We are so afraid to lose connection (and sometimes to make it), yet the deepest connection is always available when we are resting in ourselves. If we do not abandon ourselves, we cannot be abandoned. We are always already connected.

While we can and do meet others in all the objective ways I described above, an essential meeting always happens in the heart. By "essential" I mean deepest and most intimate. Yet what is this that we call the heart? When I initially investigate this "place," it feels like a center of warmth inside my chest. Think of someone you love right now and notice what you feel. If we explore this feeling more thoroughly, however, we will not find a center or periphery. This apparent meeting place dissolves. There is only openness, intimacy, and unbounded love. We discover something beyond our limited self, something universal. It is here that we most truly meet.

In order to meet others in this most intimate of ways, we must first be at home within ourselves. Our relationship with others is rooted in our relationship with ourselves. If we are not intimate with ourselves, it is impossible to be so with others. Self-intimacy comes from profound self-acceptance.

If we take ourselves to be either an inflated or a deficient somebody, we are not at home, and our contact with others will be partial. To the degree that we are trying to fill a hole in ourselves, we are not entirely at home. Nor are we at home in ourselves if we are desperate to be seen or to remain hidden. If we are lost in the fear of abandonment, attack, or engulfment, we are far from home. If we are caught in a caretaker identity—one who cares for others as an unconscious strategy to be cared for—we are also not fully at home.

The more we take ourselves and others to be objects, the further away from home we are. There seem to be endless ways to be homeless while we appear to be in a relationship! Yet, as Ramana Maharshi pointed out, we are always at home—we just don't realize it. All of the kinds of inner homelessness that I just described are forms of self-forgetfulness. As Byron Katie would say, "It is just innocent confusion."

When I am at home in myself, I meet you in and as myself. This is a step beyond Martin Buber's description of an I–Thou relationship.[1] It is I–I. This does not mean that differences are ignored or erased. There is a clear recognition, respect, and even celebration of the distinctive views, feelings, and needs of others; it is not a psychological merging. It is the recognition that the apparent "I" here and the apparent "you" there share the same ground of being. As being, you are an expression of myself. As being, I am an expression of yourself. This is true communion. In the same way that we are connected with all biological life through our shared DNA, we are connected with all of life through our shared being. We are like different trees that share the same ground. Are we the tree or the ground? Yes. We are unique and not separate—neither two nor one. These words are crude pointers to this direct, inner knowing.

The Challenge of Relationships

As I suggested in the introductory chapter, relationships tend to be the most challenging arena for spiritually oriented people. We may be fine reading our spiritual books and being on retreat, but what happens when we deal with a friend, partner, or family member with whom we are in conflict? Inner peace can fly out the window in the blink of an eye and be followed by days of inner turmoil. As a result, we may want to avoid the messy business of relationships and hole up in a monastery for a while.

We can approach human relationships as a catalyst for spiritual growth rather than an obstacle. Relationships are where the rubber hits the road, where residues of the apparently separate self get exposed and worked through. They are the launching pad for the judging mind and the laboratory for examining and withdrawing these projections. They are where we practice telling and hearing the unarguable truth. Relationships are where we test and temper the depths of our spiritual understanding.

When I recently co-led a workshop with Dorothy Hunt entitled "Meeting the Sacred in Relationship," I asked the participants what took them away from this nonplace of the heart. Everyone had variations of the same answer: judgments. Judging always creates separation.

EXPERIMENT   *Observing the Effect of Judging Others*

Think of someone whom you strongly judge. What is your judgment? Notice the feeling that it generates. Do you feel closer to or more distant from the other person? •

As I noted in chapter 4, our most frequent and charged judgments of others carry a hidden judgment of ourselves. We unconsciously project what is unwelcome in ourselves and experience it mirrored back by others. It is really quite impressive to see how our inner and outer arguments with others decline in direct proportion to our self-acceptance. As long as we think that getting others to change will make us happy, we will continue to judge and blame them. When we discover that our happiness comes from self-acceptance and self-knowledge, we stop reflexively trying to manipulate others. No one else can make us happy or unhappy. They can certainly trigger us at times, but these triggers become opportunities to examine our own reactions—our core limiting beliefs and the disturbing emotions and sensations that they induce.

This does not mean that we become passive. Rather, we become more conscious and self-responsible. When we share our subjective truth, we are willing to be honest, vulnerable, and sometimes mistaken. Our willingness and capacity to deeply listen is the greatest gift we can offer to one another.

The more open, present, and awake we are, the less objectlike our relationships become. So-called relationship becomes *relating*. The noun transforms into a verb—an apparent thing opens up into a living process. If I no longer take myself to be an object, I also cannot make you into one. Nor can I create what is happening between us into a something. We may call it friendship, but it is really a dynamic mystery, a lively, unfolding, open-ended process of listening, sharing, and discovery.

When we are no longer protecting our images and exchanging news reports over a wall, a completely new level of intimacy unfolds. Yes, I may be called your partner, friend, parent, child, sister, or brother, but if I know that I am none of these, I am available and open. If I deeply know that you are not here to fulfill me and cannot diminish me, then our meeting is a mutual sharing from fullness. Then we can truly meet in love just as we are.

CONCLUSION

the sacred ordinary

At the beginning of chapter 9, I asked where our inner knowing is leading us. It seems to me that it is leading us home—to right here—in order, as the poet suggests, to know this "place" for the first time. This place, whatever is before you in this moment, may not appear to be anything special. In fact, it will almost always look very ordinary and familiar. It is the evolutionary job of the conditioned mind to make it seem this way, since it takes less energy to categorize our experience as "known" than to really see, feel, and touch what is actually here. Thinking that we know something—transforming the unknown into the ordinary—serves our biological survival. But we are here for more than mere survival, and we are not puppets of the conditioned mind.

Our body is a trustworthy conduit of inner knowing—far more than the conditioned mind, which is so easily seduced by ideas. It is closer to the ground from which it springs and to the pulse of life. It has a remarkable capacity for felt sensing—the whole-body sense of things—the far reach of which includes our inner truth. As our body is freed from conditioned thoughts and reactive feelings, it becomes an increasingly fine-tuned instrument for being in touch with reality.

There are multiple somatic markers of inner knowing. In this book, I focused on the four most common that have emerged during tens of thousands of client sessions over the past three decades. These four—a relaxed groundedness, inner alignment, openheartedness, and spaciousness—have appeared repeatedly as I have both guided and followed hundreds of my clients and students during their unfolding process of self-discovery. Dozens of interviews with friends, students, colleagues, and former clients confirm these observations. So does my own experience.

As we tune in to our deepest nature, our body relaxes, grounds, lines up, opens up, and lights up. So far, this extraordinarily useful subtle feedback has been largely overlooked; almost nothing has been written about it. We need to both sense and decode these signals if we are to benefit from them. These bodily markers are here to be seen and used as guides to enable us to more gracefully navigate life and to awaken. They are part of our birthright, available to anyone.

Awakening does not end with the discovery of our true nature as open awareness. This is only the beginning of another process. Life also invites us to discover the true nature of our body and, by extension, the world. There is a natural movement of open, loving awareness to saturate the densest levels of form in order to meet and free the areas of greatest confusion and suffering. This movement is at the heart of the Bodhisattva vow to work for the enlightenment of all beings. It is also found in Christian teachings on the power of redemptive love and Jewish teachings of *tikkun olam* (repairing the world). Loving awareness will liberate everything it touches, if we are honest and vulnerable enough to allow it. It fosters a great intimacy.

As the body awakens, so does the world. When we discover that the core of the body is made up of empty, vibrant, and wakeful openness, we experience the world differently. The world *as other* dissolves and becomes intimate. As a result, our ordinary experience is suffused with a sense of the sacred. We discover what I like to call the sacred ordinary. We feel grateful for no reason.

This is a quiet knowing, rather than an ecstatic display of fireworks. While there may be moments of bliss and dramatic revelation along the way, this knowing brings an inner contentment and peace. Nothing is extraordinary, yet everything is sacred.

The twelfth-century Chinese Buddhist master Kakuan created a series of pictures, based on earlier Taoist teachings, that he called the "Ten Bulls." Later, in Zen, they came to be known as the "Ten Ox-Herding Pictures."[1] They describe typical steps in the discovery of our true nature—what it is to be truly human. The final picture is entitled "In the World" and depicts a little man returning to the marketplace after his long journey of searching for and taming the bull. The inscription reads:

Barefooted and naked of breast, I mingle with the people of the world. My clothes are ragged and dust-laden, and I am ever blissful. I use no magic to extend my life. Now, before me, the dead trees come alive.

Chapter 1: The Science of Attunement

1. Ainsworth, *Infancy in Uganda.*
2. Mary B. Main, "Adult Attachment Interview Protocol," from the Adult Attachment Measures Interview Library, Attachment Theory and Research at SUNY Stony Brook: resources and commentary from Everett Waters, Judith Crowell, Harriet Waters, and colleagues at SUNY Stony Brook and the New York Attachment Consortium. Available at psychology.sunysb.edu/attachment/measures/content/aai_interview.pdf. Accessed March 20, 2014.
3. Siegel, *The Mindful Therapist,* 65–6.
4. MacLean, *The Triune Brain.*
5. Damasio, *Self Comes to Mind,* 49.
6. Rizzolatti, et al., "Premotor Cortex and the Recognition of Motor Actions."
7. V. S. Ramachandran, "Mirror Neurons and Imitation Learning as the Driving Force Behind 'the Great Leap Forward' in Human Evolution," Edge 69 (May 31, 2000). Available at cogsci.ucsd.edu/~rik/courses/cogs1_w10/readings/ramachandran00.pdf. Accessed April 11, 2014. Also available at edge.org/conversation/mirror-neurons-and-imitation-learning-as-the-driving-force-behind-the-great-leap-forward-in-human-evolution. It is interesting to note that when the Italian researchers wrote up their findings and submitted an article to *Nature* for publication, it was rejected for not being "interesting enough." The same article was accepted for publication at a later date.
8. Ibid., 38.
9. Stamenov and Gallese, *Mirror Neurons.*
10. Ekman and Friesen, "Constants Across Cultures."

11. Ramachandran, "Mirror Neurons," 134.
12. Iacoboni, "Imitation, Empathy, and Mirror Neurons," 667.
13. Damasio, *Self Comes to Mind,* 195.
14. Ramachandran, "Mirror Neurons," 261.
15. Metzinger, *The Ego Tunnel.*
16. Parnia, *Erasing Death,* 223–8.
17. Siegel, *The Mindful Therapist,* 67.
18. Ibid., 54.
19. Ibid., 80.
20. Antoine Lutz, et al., "Long-Term Meditators Self-Induce High-Amplitude Gamma Synchrony during Mental Practice," Proceedings of the National Academy of Sciences 101, no. 46 (November 16, 2004): 16,369–73. Available at brainimaging. waisman.wisc.edu/~lutz/Lutz_et_al_Meditation_gamma_ EEG_2004.pdf. Accessed April 11, 2014.
21. Travis, "Comparison of Coherence, Amplitude, and eLORETA Patterns."
22. Hanson and Mendius, *Buddha's Brain,* 14.
23. "Overview of the Shamatha Project," content on the website of UC Davis Center for the Mind and Brain, webpage Labs: Saron Lab (Dr. Clifford Saron): The Shamatha Project. Available at mindbrain.ucdavis.edu/labs/Saron/shamatha-project. Accessed April 11, 2014.
24. Siegel, *The Mindful Therapist,* 127.
25. Ibid., 265.

Chapter 2: Felt Sensing and the Subtle Body

1. Gendlin and Lietaer, "On Client-Centered and Experiential Psychotherapy." Also available at focusing.org/gendlin/docs/ gol_2102.html. Accessed April 11, 2014.
2. Luke 15:20–4 (New International Version).
3. Tolle, *The Power of Now,* 105.
4. Waking down is a very useful term coined by Saniel Bonder. For more, see his website, Waking Down (wakingdown.org).

Chapter 3: Being with Experience: Shadows as Portals

1. Matthew 25:31–3, 41 (New International Version).
2. Welwood, *Toward a Psychology of Awakening.*
3. Hameed Ali (a.k.a. A. H. Almaas), the founder of the Diamond Approach, has been a pioneer in recognizing and describing this phenomenon. See *Elements of the Real in Man* (Diamond Heart, Book 1) and *The Freedom to Be* (Diamond Heart, Book 2).
4. Levine, *Waking the Tiger,* 197–9.
5. Parnell, *Attachment-Focused EMDR.*
6. For some excellent ways to develop inner resources, see Hanson, *Hardwiring Happiness;* Graham, *Bouncing Back;* Miller, *Yoga Nidra;* and Parnell, *Tapping In.*

Chapter 4: Questioning Core Beliefs, Dialoguing with the Inner Critic, and Witnessing Thoughts

1. See Katie, *Loving What Is,* and Dwoskin, *The Sedona Method.*
2. Stone and Stone, *Embracing Ourselves.*
3. Segal, *Collision with the Infinite.*

Chapter 5: Relaxed Groundedness

1. Greene, *Moral Tribes.*
2. Loy, *Lack and Transcendence,* 109.
3. Smith, *Why We Lie.*
4. "Love Returning for Itself: An Interview with Adyashanti" in Prendergast, Fenner, and Krystal, eds., *The Sacred Mirror.*
5. Tolle, *The Power of Now.*

Chapter 7: Openheartedness

1. Antonio Machado, "Last Night as I Was Sleeping," in Housden, *Ten Poems that Can Change Your Life.*
2. Johnson, *Rumi.*

Chapter 8: Spaciousness

1. Whitman, *Leaves of Grass*, 29.

Chapter 9: Self-Recognition

1. See Weber, *A Cry in the Desert*.
2. Spira, *Presence*.

Chapter 10: The Great Intimacy

1. Buber, *I and Thou*.

Conclusion: The Sacred Ordinary

1. Reps, *Zen Flesh, Zen Bones*.

bibliography

Adyashanti. *Emptiness Dancing.* Boulder, CO: Sounds True, 2006.

———. *The End of Your World: Uncensored Straight Talk on the Nature of Enlightenment.* Boulder, CO: Sounds True, 2010.

———. *Falling into Grace: Insights on the End of Suffering.* Boulder, CO: Sounds True, 2013.

———. *The Way of Liberation.* San Jose, CA: Open Gate Sangha, 2013.

Ainsworth, Mary. *Infancy in Uganda.* Baltimore: Johns Hopkins, 1967.

Almaas, A. H. *Diamond Heart,* Books 1 and 2. Boston: Shambhala, 2000.

Brach, Tara. *Radical Acceptance: Embracing Your Life with the Heart of a Buddha.* New York: Bantam, 2004.

Buber, Martin. *I and Thou.* Eastford, CT: Martino Fine Books, 2000.

Damasio, Antonio. *Self Comes to Mind: Constructing the Conscious Brain.* New York: Pantheon, 2010.

Dwoskin, Hale. *The Sedona Method: Your Key to Lasting Happiness, Success, Peace and Emotional Well-Being.* Sedona, AZ: Sedona Press, 2003.

Ekman, Paul, and W. V. Friesen. "Constants Across Cultures in the Face and Emotion." Journal of Personality and Social Psychology 17, no. 2 (1971): 124–9.

Foster, Jeff. *The Deepest Acceptance: Radical Awakening in Ordinary Life.* Boulder, CO: Sounds True, 2012.

Gendlin, Eugene. *Focusing.* New York: Bantam, 1982.

———, and G. Lietaer. "On Client-Centered and Experiential Psychotherapy: An Interview with Eugene Gendlin." In *Research on Psychotherapeutic Approaches. Proceedings of the 1st European Conference on Psychotherapy, Trier,* vol. 2, edited by W. R. Minsel and W. Herff, 77–104. Frankfurt am Main/Bern: Peter Lang, 1981.

Graham, Linda. *Bouncing Back: Rewiring Your Brain for Maximum Resilience and Well-Being.* Novato, CA: New World Library, 2013.

Greene, Joshua. *Moral Tribes: Emotion, Reason, and the Gap between Us and Them.* New York: Penguin, 2013.

Hanson, Rick. *Hardwiring Happiness: The New Brain Science of Contentment, Calm, and Confidence.* New York: Harmony, 2013.

_____. with Rick Mendius. *Buddha's Brain: The Practical Neuroscience of Happiness, Love, and Wisdom.* Oakland, CA: New Harbinger, 2009.

Housden, Roger. *Ten Poems to Change Your Life.* New York: Harmony, 2001.

Iacoboni, Marco. "Imitation, Empathy, and Mirror Neurons." *Annual Review of Psychology* 60 (2009): 653–70.

_____. *Mirroring People: The Science of Empathy and How We Connect with Others.* New York: Picador, 2008.

Johnson, Will. *Rumi: Gazing at the Beloved: The Radical Practice of Beholding the Divine.* Rochester, VT: Inner Traditions, 2003.

Katie, Byron. *Loving What Is: Four Questions That Can Change Your Life.* New York: Crown Archetype, 2002.

Klein, Jean. *Be Who You Are.* Salisbury, UK: Non-Duality Press, 2006.

_____. *The Ease of Being.* Durham, NC: Acorn Press, 1986.

_____. *Who Am I?* Salisbury, UK: Non-Duality Press, 2006.

Levertov, Denise. "The Avowal." In *The Stream and the Sapphire.* New York: New Directions, 1997.

Levine, Peter. *Waking the Tiger: Healing Trauma.* Berkeley, CA: North Atlantic, 1997.

Loy, David. *Lack and Transcendence.* Amherst, MA: Prometheus, 2000.

Lusseyran, Jacques. *And There Was Light: The Extraordinary Memoir of a Blind Hero of the French Resistance in World War II.* Novato, CA: New World Library, 2014.

MacLean, Paul. *The Triune Brain in Evolution: Role in Paleocerebral Functions.* New York: Springer, 1990.

Maharaj, Nisargadatta. *I Am That,* 2nd American ed., revised. Durham, NC: Acorn Press, 2012.

Maharshi, Ramana. *Talks with Ramana Maharshi.* San Diego: Inner Directions, 2000.

Metzinger, Thomas. *The Ego Tunnel: The Science of the Mind and the Myth of the Self.* New York: Basic Books, 2009.

Miller, Richard. *Yoga Nidra: A Meditative Practice for Deep Relaxation and Healing.* Boulder, CO: Sounds True, 2010.

Parnell, Laurel. *Attachment-Focused EMDR: Healing Relational Trauma.* New York: W. W. Norton, 2013.

_____. *Tapping In: A Step-by-Step Guide to Activating Your Healing Resources Through Bilateral Stimulation.* Boulder, CO: Sounds True, 2008.

Parnia, Sam. *Erasing Death: The Science That Is Rewriting the Boundaries Between Life and Death.* New York: HarperOne, 2013.

Prendergast, John, and Kenneth Bradford. *Listening from the Heart of Silence: Nondual Wisdom and Psychotherapy,* vol. 2. St. Paul, MN: Paragon House, 2007.

_____, Peter Fenner, and Sheila Krystal, eds. *The Sacred Mirror: Nondual Wisdom and Psychotherapy.* St. Paul, MN: Paragon House, 2003.

Ramachandran, V. S. *The Tell-Tale Brain: A Neuroscientist's Quest for What Makes Us Human.* New York: W. W. Norton, 2011.

Reps, Paul, and Nyogen Senzaki, comps. *Zen Flesh, Zen Bones.* North Clarendon, VT: Tuttle, 2008.

Rizzolatti, Giacomo, et al. "Premotor Cortex and the Recognition of Motor Actions." *Cognitive Brain Research* 3 (1996): 131–41.

Segal, Suzanne. *Collision with the Infinite: A Life Beyond the Personal Self.* San Diego: Blue Dove Press, 1996.

Siegel, Daniel J. *The Mindful Therapist.* New York: W. W. Norton, 2010.

Smith, David Livingstone. *Why We Lie: The Evolutionary Roots of Deception and the Unconscious Mind.* New York: St. Martin's Griffin, 2007.

Spira, Rupert. *Presence: The Art of Peace and Happiness,* vol. 1. Salisbury, UK: Non-Duality Press, 2011.

_____. *Presence: The Intimacy of All Experience,* vol. 2. Salisbury, UK: Non-Duality Press, 2011.

Stamenov, Maxim, and Vittorio Gallese, eds. *Mirror Neurons and the Evolution of Brain and Language.* Amsterdam: John Benjamins, 2002.

Stone, Hal, and Sidra Stone. *Embracing Ourselves: The Voice Dialogue Manual.* Novato, CA: New World Library, 1998.

Tolle, Eckhart. *The Power of Now.* Novato, CA: New World Library, 2004.

Travis, Fred. "Comparison of Coherence, Amplitude, and eLORETA Patterns during Transcendental Meditation and TM-Sidhi Practice." *International Journal of Psychophysiology* 81 no. 3 (2011): 198–202.

Weber, Christin Lore. *A Cry in the Desert: The Awakening of Byron Katie.* Lancaster, CA: The Work Foundation, 1996.

Welwood, John. *Toward a Psychology of Awakening: Buddhism, Psychotherapy, and the Path of Personal and Spiritual Transformation.* Boston: Shambhala, 2002.

Whitman, Walt. *Leaves of Grass and Other Writings.* New York: W. W. Norton, 2002.

acknowledgments

I am particularly grateful to my two main readers: Marjorie Bair, whose encouragement and fine-tuned feedback was extremely helpful, and Steve Hadland, whose critical eye and aesthetic sensitivity ("less Henry James, more Hemingway!") helped me to pare down the text and more clearly express myself. A special thanks as well to Stephan Bodian and Kelly Boys for their enthusiastic support and interest as they read through the entire manuscript.

Amy Rost, my editor at Sounds True, brought rigorous clarity and meticulous attention to help sculpt the final form of this work. A deep bow to her and to the entire Sounds True team!

This book would never have gotten off the ground without the encouragement of Daniel Ellenberg, who suggested that we start a writing group with James Baraz, Karen Buckley, and Jeanne-Marie Grumet, each of whom helped this project along.

I am also grateful to those who consented to be interviewed about their bodily sense of inner knowing—Adyashanti, Stephan Bodian, Saniel and Linda Bonder, Debira Branscombe, Silke and John Greiner, Rick Hanson, Dorothy Hunt, Lee Klinger Lesser, Premsiri Lewin, Tiaga Liner, Richard Miller, Riyaz Motan, Lama Palden, Laurel Parnell, Christiane Prendergast, Lily Sun, and David Wise, as well as to those who responded to written questionnaires—Marjorie Bair, Dan Berkow, Judith Blackstone, Arthur Giacalone, and Mike Hock.

I am very grateful to my wife, Christiane, whose generous and steady support while I was sequestered in my study for weekends and sometimes weeks allowed for this eighteen-month birthing process.

Many thanks as well to my clients who let their stories be told as an inspiration for others.

index

expression of, 114–15
foreground stage of, 176
the four stage continuum of
   groundedness and, 112–21
infinite, 114–15
locating, 24
loving, 190
spacious, 165–68
spaciousness and, 159
wakeful, 96
witnessing of thoughts and, 94–96

the backward step, 175
Bankei, 70
becoming, 129–30
being
   being awareness, 94–95
   with experience, 57–77
   as you are, 66–67, 69–70
beliefs, xii, 1
   core, 79, 81–87, 96, 159–60
   limiting, xxi, 49, 55, 85–87, 96,
     159–60
   questioning, 73, 79, 81–87, 96, 137
   recognizing, 96
   uncovering through somatic and
     emotional reactions, 82–83
the belly, 33, 35–37. *See also* the *hara*
Blackstone, Judith, 164
Blake, William, *The Marriage of Heaven
   and Hell,* 49
blindness, 144–46
Bodhisattva, 190
Bodian, Stephan, 164
the body. *See also* body identity
   agency of, 17, 18–19
   felt sensing and, 30
   as form par excellence, 181
   identifying with, 160–61
   inner knowing and, 28, 189–90
   listening to, xvi, xvii–xviii, 127–28
   modeling of, 17–18
   objective view of, 1–53
   ownership of, 17, 18–19
   perspective of, 17, 18–19
   self and, 17–19, 36
   self-attunement and, 20–21

sensing, 20–21, 28, 82–83, 161–62,
   163
sensitivity of, 1, 173–74
simulation and, 17–18
subjective view of, 1–53
two views of, 1–53
body identity, the four stage continuum
   of groundedness and, 110–22, *110*
Bonder, Saniel, 194n4
bonding, 5–9, 183–87
book of Luke, 34–35
boundaries, 52
Bowlby, John, 7
Brahms, Johannes, 94
brain
   evolutionary layers of the, 10
   limbic (paleomammalian), 10
   neocortex, 10
   reptilian, 10
brain-wave synchrony, 22–23
Brancombe, Debira, 127, 165
Buber, Martin, 185
Buddha's Brain (Hanson), 23
Buddhism, 190–91. *See also* Tibetan
   Buddhism; Zen Buddhism
bypassing, 68–69

Cambodia, 88
the central channel, the chakras and,
   38–39
the chakras, 35. *See also* energy centers
   the central channel and, 38–39
   clarity, 48–50
   the energy body and, 37–38
   exploring, 40–42
   fifth chakra, 46–48
   first chakra, 40–42, 52
   fourth chakra, 44–46, 52
   heart chakra, 52, 126
   honest self-expression, 46–48
   interpersonal power, 43–44
   love, 44–46
   root chakra, 118 (*see also* first chakra)
   safety, 40–42
   second chakra, 42–43, 52
   sensuality, 42–43

inner reconciliation, 90, 97
inner resonance, discovering, xx–xxi
inner self-helper (ISH), 104
inner space, discovering, 159–66
insights
  spontaneous, 93–94
  transformative, 29
integrated coherence, 22, 26
integration, 26
  FACES of, 22
integrity, 132–34, 137
  sensing being out of, 134
interconnectedness, xiii–xiv
interoception, 20–21, 26, 31
interpersonal power, 43–44
intimacy, xxi, 190
  the great intimacy, 183–87
  merging and, 168–69
  spacious, 167–69
intuition, xii
I-Thou relationship, 185

Jesus, 34–35
Judaism, 190
judgments, 88–89, 93, 96–97, 160,
  186–87. See also inner critic
  observing, 83
Jung, Carl, 57

Kabat-Zinn, Jon, 65
Kakuan, 190–91
Kashmiri Shaivism, xiv
Katie, Byron, 178, 185
  "The Work," 84
kindness, 135
King, Martin Luther Jr., 135
Klein, Jean, xiv, xx, 27, 33, 70, 95,
  129–30, 136, 173, 175, 176,
  178–79, 181
knowing, inner. See inner knowing
Kornfield, Jack, 65
kundalini, 39

Lannon, Richard, *The General Theory of Love*, 10–11
"Last Night as I Was Sleeping" (Machado), 148
letting go, 118–20, 122, 165, 178
Levertov, Denise, "The Avowal," 108–9
Levine, Peter, 76
Lewis, Thomas, *The General Theory of Love*, 10–11
limbic (paleomammalian) brain, 10
limbic regulation, 11
limbic resonance, early theory of, 10–11
limbic revision, 11
limiting beliefs, xxi, 49, 55, 159–60
  core, 81
  identifying, 81
  inquiry into, 85–87
  questioning, 96
  recognizing, 96
  sensing the impact of, 82
Linehan, Marcia, 65
listening
  to the body, xvi, xvii–xviii, 127–28
  deep, 68
  inner, xxi, 25
  true, 38
loneliness, 73–74
Longchenpa, 157
love, 44–46, 154, 185
  attunement and, 154
loving-kindness, 22
Loy, David, 105
Lusseyran, Jacques, *And There Was Light*, 144–46
Lutz, Antoine, 22

Machado, Antonio, "Last Night as I Was Sleeping," 148
MacLean, Paul D., 10
Maharaj, Nisargadatta, 174
  I Am That, xiv
Maharshi, Ramana, 139, 174, 185
Main, Mary, 7–9

reality, x, xix, xx, 17, 22, 24, 34, 46, 49, 69, 87, 93, 96, 132, 135, 189
groundedness and, 110, 117–18, 122
maps of, 92, 97
models of, 102
as pure awareness, 125
thoughts and, 96, 97
receiving, 30
reconciliation, inner, 90, 97
relating, 187
relationships, challenge of, 186–87
relaxation, 66–67, 74, 164. *See also* relaxed groundedness
core, 102–5, 121, 165
relaxed groundedness, xxi, 99, 101, 171, 189
attuning with, *122*
release, 165
relief, 165
reptilian brain, 10
resistance, 65–66
resonance, 21, 133, 176
emotional, 4
inner knowing and, 21–25
as mutual attunement, 21
resonating, 30
restlessness, 177
"right now," contemplating, 93
Rizzolatti, Giacomo, 12
Rogers, Carl, 28
root chakra, 52, 118. *See also* first chakra
rubber-hand illusion, 17–19, 25
Rumi, 94
ruminating, 33–34

sadness, 57–58
safety, 40–42
Sai Baba, xiii
samadhi, 92
Sambhogakaya, 38
satyagraha, 135
Scharlack, Dan, 113

scientific investigation, of attunement, 4–5
second chakra, 42–43, 52
secure attachment style, 7
Sedona Method, 84
Segal, Suzanne, 91–92
self
the body and, 17–19, 36
feelings of knowing and, 17
illusion of, 104–5
as a product of brain functioning, 19
sense of, 36
self-acceptance, 146–48, 154, 185, 187
self-attunement, 16–19, 26
the body and, 20–21
self-care, 154
self-criticism. *See* inner critic
self-doubt, xi
self-expression, honest, 46–48
self-identity, 18–19
self-image, 103–6, 121, 125, 134
self-inquiry, 50, 175
self-intimacy, 185
self-knowing, 5
self-love, 7, 146–48, 154
self-recognition, xxi, 173
self-responsibility, 47
self-trust, xvi, 178–80
sensations, 99, 137, 174
sensing, 72
sensing, inside the body, 20–21
sensitivity, 52
sensory markers, xxi
sensuality, 42–43
separation, illusion of, 96
serpent energy, 39
seventh chakra, 50–51, 52
shadows, as portals, 58–64, 77
Shamatha Project, 23
shame, xviii
Siegel, Daniel, 7–9, 21, 23–25, 26, 31, 65, 161
The Mindful Therapist, 20–22

John J. Prendergast, PhD, has been working as a psychotherapist for over three decades. He is a recently retired professor of psychology at the California Institute of Integral Studies, where he taught and supervised graduate counseling students since 1989. He is the senior editor of and contributor to two anthologies of original essays, *The Sacred Mirror: Nondual Wisdom and Psychotherapy* (2003; with Peter Fenner and Sheila Krystal) and *Listening from the Heart of Silence* (2007; with Ken Bradford). He is the cofounder and current advisor to the annual Conference on Nonduality and Psychology, and the editor-in-chief of *Undivided: The Online Journal of Nonduality and Psychology* (undividedjournal.com). He studied for many years with the European Advaita master Dr. Jean Klein, and with Adyashanti. In 2012 he was invited to share the dharma by Dorothy Hunt. He lives in Petaluma, California. For more, please visit listeningfromsilence.com.

about sounds true

Sounds True is a multimedia publisher whose mission is to inspire and support personal transformation and spiritual awakening. Founded in 1985 and located in Boulder, Colorado, we work with many of the leading spiritual teachers, thinkers, healers, and visionary artists of our time. We strive with every title to preserve the essential "living wisdom" of the author or artist. It is our goal to create products that not only provide information to a reader or listener, but that also embody the quality of a wisdom transmission.

For those seeking genuine transformation, Sounds True is your trusted partner. At SoundsTrue.com you will find a wealth of free resources to support your journey, including exclusive weekly audio interviews, free downloads, interactive learning tools, and other special savings on all our titles.

To learn more, please visit SoundsTrue.com/freegifts or call us toll-free at 800-333-9185.